Bold Partnership for a New Generation

NOT YOUR PARENTS' MARRIAGE

Jerome & Kellie Daley

WATERBROOK
PRESS

NOT YOUR PARENTS' MARRIAGE
PUBLISHED BY WATERBROOK PRESS
12265 Oracle Boulevard, Suite 200
Colorado Springs, Colorado 80921
A division of Random House, Inc.

All Scripture quotations, unless otherwise indicated, are taken from the Holy Bible, New International Version®. NIV®. Copyright © 1973, 1978, 1984 by International Bible Society. Used by permission of Zondervan Publishing House. All rights reserved. Scripture quotations marked (KJV) are taken from the King James Version. Scripture quotations marked (MSG) are taken from The Message by Eugene H. Peterson. Copyright © 1993, 1994, 1995, 1996, 2000, 2001, 2002. Used by permission of NavPress Publishing Group. All rights reserved. Scripture quotations marked (NASB) are taken from the New American Standard Bible®. © Copyright The Lockman Foundation 1960, 1962, 1963, 1968, 1971, 1972, 1973, 1975, 1977, 1995. Used by permission. (www.Lockman.org).

Italics in Scripture quotations indicate the authors' added emphasis.

Names and certain identifying details in some anecdotes and stories have been changed to protect the identities of the persons involved.

ISBN 1-57856-896-X

Library of Congress Cataloging-in-Publication Data
Daley, Jerome.
  Not your parents' marriage : recovering God's unique design for lifelong partnership / Jerome and Kellie Daley. — 1st ed.
      p. cm.
  Includes bibliographical references.
  ISBN 1-57856-896-X (alk. paper)
  1. Marriage—Religious aspects—Christianity. I. Daley, Kellie. II. Title.
  BV835.D35 2006
  248.8'44—dc22

                                      2006008982

Printed in the United States of America
2006—First Edition

10 9 8 7 6 5 4 3 2 1

Praise for
Not Your Parents' Marriage

"I wish I'd had this book when my husband and I got married! It would have spared us a lot of misunderstandings. *Not Your Parents' Marriage* should be required reading for every couple who wants to have the kind of marriage God intends."

> —GINGER KOLBABA, managing editor of *Marriage Partnership* magazine and author of *Surprised by Remarriage*

"Jerome and Kellie Daley welcome us to grow in our marriages by inviting us into their own discoveries of partnership in marriage. They provide helpful, practical suggestions for developing partnership together, appreciating each other's God-given gifts, and consequently experiencing God's fullest blessings in marriage."

> —CRAIG S. KEENER, professor of New Testament at Palmer Theological Seminary and author of the best-selling *IVP Bible Background Commentary: New Testament*

"The Daleys give you a glimpse into their marriage, from the early days filled with presumption to the realities of marriage in today's society. They deal with the relevant issues affecting couples today, including fresh insights into the roles of men and women in marriage. I highly recommend *Not Your Parents' Marriage* for all who want a marriage that is pleasing to God and highly satisfying to the couple!"

> —BARBARA WENTROBLE, founder of International Breakthrough Ministries and author of *Prophetic Intercession, Praying with Authority,* and *Rise to Your Destiny*

Praise for
When God Waits

"Jerome Daley explains the value of faithfully doing what we know to do until God reveals the next step.... If you're longing for God to open up your destiny, read this book. *When God Waits* is a much-needed gift to all who have ever wished that God would just hurry up!"

—TED HAGGARD, author of *The Jerusalem Diet* and president of the National Association of Evangelicals

"In *When God Waits*, Jerome Daley probes one of God's more frustrating habits: promising a hope and a future, and then hanging fire. What is God waiting for? Daley, in search of an answer, quarries several stories from Scripture as well as his own season of limbo and emerges with a reminder of the riches hidden within divine delay."

—MARK BUCHANAN, author of *The Rest of God* and *The Holy Wild*

"Jerome Daley has extended an irresistible invitation to those of us who sometimes find ourselves desperately clinging to the hope that there's a purpose in life's disappointments and difficulties. *When God Waits* is written by someone who, having endured the darkness, has become resolute in his belief that God is unrelentingly good and outrageously in love with us."

—FIL ANDERSON, author of *Running on Empty*

"*When God Waits* provides a landing place for the confusion and disillusionment that come from seasons of seeming inactivity on the part of God. Jerome Daley has done my heart a service through this beautiful work, encouraging me that the waiting is actually doing something in me, is actually taking me somewhere good."

—JAN MEYERS, author of *The Allure of Hope* and *Listening to Love*

NOT YOUR PARENTS'
marriage

We would like to dedicate this book to our parents,
Margaret and Frank Wilder and Nan and Jerry Daley,
who have modeled much of God's heart in their marriages
and have deposited much into our marriage through prayer and wisdom.
Both where their perspectives are identical to ours and where they are different,
they have encouraged and supported our passion to build marriage partnerships
throughout the generations.
We will always be grateful for your love, your parenting,
and your friendship.

contents

preface

MARRIAGE IS TOUGH. And glorious. And perplexing and exhilarating and, well...you name it! Marriage is both the core and microcosm of most people's adult existence. It is ours.

In writing this book, we want to invite you into a sacred place in our hearts. We want to be transparently real about the things we have learned as well as the things we have yet to learn about marriage. Some things we have learned by accident, stumbling over obvious realities that had somehow eluded us. Other things we have learned by watching. Some of our most compelling convictions were birthed in times of great difficulty—in the stabbing pain of angry words and raised voices or the dull ache of prolonged misunderstandings.

But after fifteen years of togetherness, we have begun to experience a level of joy in our partnership that amazes and satisfies us like nothing else. Interwoven through our souls, our bodies, and our spirits is a union that defies logic. It can only be explained by divine intention. And divine intervention. It's a beautiful thing.

The state of our marriage at any given time is the bellwether of our lives. If we're in harmony with each other and with God, then we know that we're well centered for anything that life may throw at us. If we're not…well, life devolves into great strain and striving. It is possible to make a god out of your marriage and let it compete for God's place in your heart. But more common is a growing neglect, an unintentional falling into patterns and forms that hamstring the potential and frustrate the glory God intends to reveal in this sacred place.

This book grew out of our story, and we hope it will illumine and clarify your story. We have tried to create a warm, comfortable setting that transcends ink on paper. Somehow, we'd like to transport you into our family room, with mugs of steaming coffee in hand and a fire burning in the fireplace. Okay, so they're gas logs, but you get the idea. We have written this book the way we live—not all pretty and neat but full of genuine encouragement, pointing toward a dream of oneness that is the nearest window into heavenly intimacy that exists this side of eternity.

Parts of this book are simply us talking. We have wrestled with ideas related to marriage for years, and as we began writing, we divided our ideas into several topics. Then we set out a tape recorder and, well, talked. What you'll see in the chapters that follow is pretty authentic to us, with minimal editing. We're not experts (we don't think there really *are* any), but we are passionate about God's invitation to partnership in this mysterious, intoxicating union called marriage.

The topics we raise are intended to provoke your own quest for truth and life in your marriage. We will likely raise more questions than we answer. In fact, part of our conviction is that each marriage has to work out its own practices in the light of the biblical vision. You can learn from our experiences and from those of others, but in the final analysis, you and your spouse will have to carve out your own path in a way that honors God and fits your souls.

In places, we'll discuss facets of marriage that are overlooked in some

Christian models. In other places, we'll bump and thrash against core ideas that men and women have bumped and thrashed against for millenniums. Of particular interest is the tension that arises as biblical marriage evolves in its methodology from generation to generation and as biblical vision is uniquely applied within the postmodern generation. Some may react negatively to this idea, but that's okay; tension is necessary for growth. It is our hope that this book will be fun and lighthearted, even as we deal with the weighty issues of partnership in marriage.

This journey into partnership began for us about six years ago, well into our married life. It started, as really important changes usually begin, as a terrifying quaking of terra firma that initially had us fearing for our very survival. After nine fairly quiet, predictable years of marriage and ministry, an explosion shook our world to its foundation. Within three months, every secure place in our lives was gone—our job, our home, our church, our income, and many of our core relationships. This is a story in its own right, and most of it is told in my (Jerome's) book *Soul Space*.

What hasn't been told is the story of our marriage and how, when the earth finally stopped its violent convulsions…and the aftershocks began to fade, we found that the cracks spiderwebbing our world had revealed something previously hidden. Buried treasure, in fact. A new life for our impoverished relationship. It was just a beginning, but what a beginning it was. This is the story and the meaning we want to share with you. So pull up a comfortable chair, grab a fresh cappuccino, and let's begin.

Getting a Clue on God's
Design for Marriage

HONORING THE PAST
WHILE MOVING PAST IT

Navigating the Generational Shift in Marriage

"WHO WANTS TO DRIVE?" A voice piped up from the circle of grad students in front of the dorm. I took off in a jog to the parking lot a quarter mile away and returned in my gunmetal gray Isuzu Trooper. Trying to live up to the rugged, adventurous image of my truck, I chirped the tires as I approached the swelling crowd of guys and girls awaiting a ride to the ice-cream store.

I (Jerome) had been on the seminary campus for only a week, and I was relishing all the new experiences and faces that made up the tight-knit community of five hundred in this South Carolina sauna called Columbia. Girls and guys started piling into my SUV, and finally the front passenger door opened. *No, it can't be! Things like this only happen in movies.* But there she was—an auburn-haired beauty I had met just briefly before. She slid into her seat with surprising grace, which wasn't so easy in this high-mounted truck.

I think that's the thing I noticed first about Kellie...well, okay, maybe not the first thing but close: she had this quiet grace about her. Nothing snooty or put-on, it was patently authentic. What do you call it...bearing? poise? To me it communicated that she was a lady, that she had confidence and self-respect. It also represented something of a subtle challenge...the man who would win her affection would have to earn it.

That's where it began for us, a blurred rocket ride that moved us faster than the speed of thought to the steps of Kellie's home church a mere six months later—where time slowed to a surreal slow motion as I slid a golden band on the third finger of her left hand.

Wow.

Now, fifteen years later, we are very different people than the ones who squeaked out those celestial vows. Did we have even a clue then? Yeah, a clue...but not much more.

How do you begin such an uncharted life? Getting married is at the same time the most natural and the most foreign step most of us

---

Better Decisions

Think about any "nondecisions" you have made as a couple. How did not making a decision together affect your relationship?

_____

_____

_____

_____

_____

_____

ever take. What do you honestly have to go on? Besides the premarital workbook that you may have scribbled in incoherently in your love-drug buzz, where do you find guidance for the specific shape of your relationship? Even within a Christian context, how are you supposed to understand this mysterious creation called marriage?

And once you're past the initial giddy awkwardness of it all, the question is still a valid one: what shape should your marriage take? What is the connection between the marriage you observed growing up and your unique shape as a couple? Should you follow your parents' example, or should you work hard at doing things differently? When you find that things aren't working, is it possible that you're stuck in structures and mind-sets that God never intended for you and your spouse to adopt? What are God's specific intentions for *your* marriage?

Marriage is the quest that takes you beyond the forms of your parents' relationship—no matter how good or bad—and into your own destiny, held in the heart of God and waiting to be unwrapped by you.

IN THE BEGINNING WAS...CONFUSION

[Jerome] Let's start with where we began. Our marriage was born in a
    wonderful, romantic fog of excitement and anticipation. But
    within just a few months we had lost the foundation of one-
    ness that is now so central to our vision of marriage. Inadver-
    tently and subconsciously, I had already made a lot of decisions
    for our new life together before we were even married.
[Kellie] That's what I now find so hard to believe—that we didn't
    discuss our plans more. We were so in love we thought that
    everything would be okay, that everything would work itself

out. We didn't think—or at least *I* didn't think—we needed
to evaluate or question our future. It's funny…I don't even
remember talking about it!

[Jerome] I think the thing we talked about most was that I wanted to
continue my job as worship pastor at my local church…that it
would be a great place for us to start our life together.

[Kellie] I don't even remember having *that* conversation! I think you
felt that way because you were already doing it—you were
already on staff, already leading the college group and leading
worship. I got excited that we could lead the campus ministry
together. That was what I envisioned for us.

That's the way my head works: It's hard for me to think
ahead and figure out how I'm going to feel about something or
what it's going to look like until I'm actually in that situation.

[Jerome] Yeah, we sort of stumbled through all these "nondecisions"
in our new life together. We had premarital counseling, but
our minds were clouded by idealistic images that were discon-
nected from the grittier realities of life. We didn't formulate a
plan for our new life or even our first year. Marriage is just so
different, so "other" than anything we'd experienced before. It
was hard to know what to anticipate.

Maybe you can relate. Marriage might have seemed like a simple thing, a
natural next step. You were so in love that you couldn't imagine not spend-
ing your lives together. And the details of being married—or, more specifically, what it meant for you and your spouse to live in the unique
relationship that God called you to—was given little thought.

Or marriage might have seemed just the opposite to you. Perhaps the models of marriage you had observed growing up lacked love and permanence, and the things that went into a good marriage were a mystery to you. So the idea of thinking intentionally about your marriage and how you wanted to fashion it was a daunting venture.

Either way, entering into marriage without thinking through and discussing the particulars of the marriage is common. And it's only later that people realize that more intentional work is needed.

THE DAMAGE OF NONDECISIONS

[Kellie] So we got married and moved back to North Carolina to get settled, and you decided you didn't want to do the college ministry after all.

[Jerome] A classic blunder…at least in the sense that we didn't make the decision together. Looking back on it, I can see that I was afraid I would fail. The college setting seemed a lot more "dangerous" to me than ministering inside the church.

[Kellie] A specific example of this decision-making dynamic was when we first moved to town. We lived that first month with your parents, who had a wonderful guest room over their garage. You were sick with strep throat, so opportunities for apartment hunting were limited. We did eventually find our own place—what seemed to be the best thing going in our price range—but I wasn't quite ready to make a decision.

That weekend we were going to my parents' house, and you felt strongly that we needed to go ahead and put down a deposit and sign the lease so we wouldn't lose the place. I wanted to take the weekend to pray over the decision, but we went ahead and signed before we left town. I wasn't upset with you, but I wasn't comfortable with the decision.

The very next day we got a call from a lady in our church. She owned a very nice townhouse that was suddenly vacant, and she offered to rent it to us for a fraction of its worth.

[Jerome] That townhouse was more than we could have dreamed of. It was a situation where God was determined to bless us beyond our wisdom or foresight. But I guess the point is that if we had been committed to making decisions together—as we are now—we wouldn't have made the blunder. We wouldn't have lost the deposit on the apartment.

But we learned from that. Now we don't make any decision of consequence that affects the other without consulting each other…without having the chance to really process it and truly come into authentic agreement.

[Kellie] Psalm 133 talks about being in unity and how that is where God commands the blessing. When you're not in unity, it's harder for God to bring that blessing.

God's overwhelming desire is to bless each of you and to bless your marriage. But he wants to bless you in a way that will build his larger design for your marriage. If you move in unity, that brings his heart and intention to bear on your marriage. God blesses your efforts to move forward together as you take each other into account and seek agreement in all your major decisions. When you fail to move in unity, you risk forfeiting God's blessing.

CONFLICTING OPINIONS AND AN EMERGING PARTNERSHIP

[Kellie] It was a hard awakening for us. You wanted so much to be a godly leader, and we learned early on that I had discernment and strong opinions. So it took us awhile to make those things mesh. It was messy at first.

[Jerome] It was a process of discovery. I certainly didn't know when we got married how strong your opinions were—or that it was a positive thing. At least it's a positive thing now that we've come to understand it and channel it through our partnership. But for a long time it didn't appear to be a good thing at all. There were times I felt you didn't respect my leadership because you wouldn't just let me make the decisions! And that was faulty thinking on my part.

[Kellie] The way marriages often unfold is either a strong husband doing the leading or, at the other end of the spectrum, a strong wife doing the leading. Intuitively, we didn't want either of those, but we defaulted to the husband-driven model because we thought it was biblical.

[Jerome] That was more faulty thinking. The biblical framework for marriage is *oneness;* that's the grid through which we have to understand leadership.

Everyone talks about oneness in marriage, but what does that really mean? What does it look like, and how do couples live it out? An older couple helped us understand a simple truth: until we come into complete agreement, we should delay making a decision. Sometimes this takes more time, but it's always worth the wait.

Oneness is the heart of marriage, and it's at the heart of God's desire for your marriage. But there is a danger in talking about oneness, because the word has lost much of its deeper meaning. That's why we've chosen instead to use the word *partnership*. It's much easier to talk about what it means to live together as partners; *oneness* seems too ethereal.

The words *oneness* and *partnership* both attempt to describe the mystical union of two people who enter marriage. *Oneness* highlights the single identity of the covenantal relationship. *Partnership* highlights the reality that this covenant will always be comprised of two distinct souls. In this sense, partnership is a practical way of looking at how two people bring their individuality into one vision, one purpose, and one destiny. Oneness is the goal; partnership is the means to that goal.

Finding Your Shared Destiny

Even among young adults, it's common to believe that it's the man's job to find his calling from God and then to find the woman he thinks should be his wife. He brings the woman into his world and says, essentially, "This is my calling. Can you be a part of it?" It's not always stated that directly, but there is the expectation that she will join his calling. There is little awareness of a shared calling and very little pursuit of what God is calling them to do *together*. When we met and got married, we didn't see our life's calling as a shared calling. Perhaps you didn't, either.

This grows out of a misunderstanding of Genesis 2, which we'll look at more closely later. But the germ of it is that in Genesis 1, God gave a mandate and spoke a destiny over Adam and Eve *as a couple*. It came to them jointly, as equal partners in destiny. And that gives context to the anchor verse for marriage, Genesis 2:24 (MSG): "Therefore a man leaves his father and mother and embraces his wife. They become one flesh." Whatever marriage is, it's about oneness! It isn't that the man has a destiny and the woman is left either to join in or to choose not to marry the guy. Instead, it's *their* destiny—given by God to both of them. The way you understand what *together* means will largely determine how you live out your marriage.

Your life together will also be shaped by the unique blend of your personalities and your gifting. Marriage isn't meant to look the same in every generation. In some ways your marriage may look very similar to your parents' marriage, and in other ways it may look completely different. Even within your own generation, the marriage relationship is meant to have a unique expression for every couple.

But oneness—living together in complete partnership—is the one nonnegotiable. God wants to take you to the highest level of oneness possible! Partnership does not mean that a man comes to his sense of destiny and then finds a woman to support his vision and care for his needs. Partnership means that God brings the two *together* to become one. A man and a woman were created specifically for each other, and when God aligns their paths, they have a shared destiny that they can fulfill only with each other. At the moment of their joining, their new, shared destiny is birthed.

If a couple fails to understand the shared nature of their destiny, God's blessing in their lives will be hindered.

[Jerome] Destiny can't be discovered outside of community. Of
  course we are born as individuals, and we come into a sense
  of personal purpose related to who we are meant to be before

marriage—the real Jerome and the real Kellie. These are fore-shadowings of destiny.

[Kellie] I would call that self-discovery—the process of discovering who we are as individuals. For instance, when we come into marriage, we should already know our spiritual gifts, our strengths and weaknesses, and what motivates us. It's so much easier for God to communicate destiny to a husband and wife when they already know who they are.

[Jerome] Part of the beauty of marriage is that once God brings two people together, not only do they begin to discover their joint destiny, but they help each other to see the blind spots they have toward themselves. It's like looking into a mirror; you begin to see things about yourself that you didn't realize before. And that aids the process of understanding yourself and becoming who you are meant to be. But the further along we are on that journey *before* we get married, the more quickly we are able to build a healthy marriage.

A Wrinkle in Time

We hope that self-discovery and a shared destiny appeal to you. But it's possible that your parents have pursued very different priorities in their marriage. In between any two generations there usually is a shift in expectations, goals, priorities, and core desires for marriage. That's why it's important to look at your marriage in terms of what God is doing today; don't try to squeeze your relationship into a model that fit a past generation.

God has given each of us a past to draw from, whether it was largely healthy or highly dysfunctional or somewhere in between. Marriages you observed while growing up, both positive and negative, tend to serve as defining models for your marriage. Most couples either try to replicate a marriage they admire, or they try to fashion the exact opposite of a destructive relationship they were exposed to.

The truth is you can learn from both the good and the bad that you observed in your parents' marriage (or *marriages,* as the case may be). We want to emphasize an attitude of honor toward the heritage we received. So as you look at your past, identify what should be honored, whether little or much. Honor and respect that and build on it. But don't allow your marriage to be completely defined by it.

God's purposes and basic principles for marriage *don't change,* but the applications and expressions of those biblical values *change constantly* and emerge in unique ways in every generation. In past generations husbands were marked by feeling a keen responsibility to provide for their families. That is honorable, and it produced generations of hard workers.

And while we honor the hard work and the deep sense of financial responsibility of those fathers, we also understand that they often had a very different idea of what it meant to be a father. Some men equated being a father primarily with being a provider, so many of these fathers were emotionally and physically distant from their children. Rearing the kids was thought to be the mother's responsibility. Fortunately, God has been calling husbands and wives to a wider understanding of his heart for how parents—both fathers and mothers—nurture their children and care for each other. This is just one example of how God continually reveals more of his heart over time.

Both Kellie and I grew up in exceptional homes where our parents loved each other, loved their children, and modeled a desire for God's rule in the family. My parents broke new ground at the time by carefully guarding a weekly family night where we all played games, read books, and just hung out together. Kellie's parents intentionally limited their careers in the education field so they could give their family the best portion of their time and attention. Both families had the extraordinary foresight to recognize the heavy cost of allowing television to rule the home…and banned televisions from their houses! As a result, we both grew up interacting with our families instead of plugging in to the mind-numbing effect of the boob tube.

Our fathers have faithfully honored and cherished their wives for more than forty years. Our mothers have loved and respected their husbands, served the church, and nurtured their children. Our parents led us into a personal discovery of Jesus Christ and the pursuit of his purpose for our lives. They taught us the value of personal purity and elevated our vision for marriage. This is the depth of the heritage we brought to our marriage.

And beyond our parents, we inherited a deep contribution from prior generations. The last several generations modeled a tremendous commitment to work, community, and family. Their industry set an honorable example of sacrificing their own resources and ambitions for the sake of their children and their children's children. My (Jerome's) grandfather, Hugh Daley, worked myriads of jobs in small businesses until he made enough money to buy his first hotel. Through wise investments and a Spartan lifestyle, he built his own company, from which he has tithed and given generously all his life.

Every generation seeks to

♀ ♀ ♀ ♀ ♀ ♀
Hers

In what significant ways is your marriage different from that of your parents? Are you okay with the differences? Are they?

_____

_____

_____

_____

_____

right the "wrongs" of the past generation, both real and perceived. But each new generation also builds on the foundations that have been carefully fought for and defended. We owe a great debt to our parents, our grandparents, and all the generations who brought us to this moment.

GOD'S HEART FOR GENERATIONS

Every generation has its own divine purpose, and God always tries to restore and redeem certain things in certain generations. Paul described King David's role from an interesting perspective: "When David had served God's purpose in his own generation, he fell asleep" (Acts 13:36). The destiny of Israel's greatest king can't be understood outside the unique context of his particular generation. And so it is today. A new set of values and priorities emerges with each generation. And some generational currents affect all of society, Christian or not. Those currents need to be looked at critically: they either reinforce Kingdom values, or, alternately, they cut across the Kingdom and confront it.

This is a challenge for both the older generations and the younger: the prior generation needs to avoid automatically rejecting cultural shifts, and the new generation needs to moderate the urge to automatically embrace every new

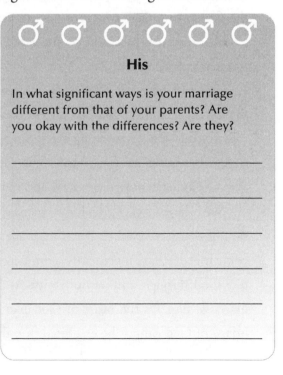

His

In what significant ways is your marriage different from that of your parents? Are you okay with the differences? Are they?

_____

_____

_____

_____

_____

current. Both generations should expect culture to change and should look for the Kingdom opportunities that emerge within those changes.

This is the bigger, zoomed-out context in which we look at biblical marriage. God wants to express himself through marriage in a way that demonstrates his heart for the world. We see God stamping upon today's generation a new and broader sense of partnership. It's not new in the sense that other generations didn't have a similar vision, but it's new in the depth and breadth of expression that is beginning to mark today's young men and women.

This is not to elevate one generation above another…or to elevate people at all. It's God's idea and initiative, and it's God's glory that is at stake. It's to his honor that Kingdom values are revealed in lives and marriages! God intends to unveil the values of community, equality, and partnership, not *exclusively* in marriage, but *uniquely* in marriage. And as God does this, the face of marriage will take on the radiance of heaven itself and will advance the cause of Christ on the earth. This is part of God's destiny for this generation.

The past generation has worked to protect the sanctity of marriage in the midst of a culture that has torn at the holiness and beauty of marriage. Our spiritual Enemy is doing everything in his power to undermine marriage. The church has fought to defend the rightful place of marriage at the core of God's heart for his people and the world.

We believe God's vision for partnership gives shape to the sacred dimension of marriage. God designed marriage for one man and one woman to come together, and together they bring a completeness that mirrors an infinite God through a finite humanity. As a man and woman become one, marriage displays the heart of God like nothing else on earth. The full image of God cannot be exhibited in only one gender; it takes both man and woman (see Genesis 1:26–27; 2:24).[1]

God does call some to remain single, and when he does, his purposes require that person to live within a very strong community of Christians. God said it's not good for men (or women) to be alone. We know that from direct experience. Our souls long for a soul mate; we long to be known, to be understood, and to be loved. Marriage is about a man and a woman coming together completely…and that togetherness is sacred. That is holy.

ONENESS IS EXCLUSIVE

It's not as though you can come together for five years and then say, "Well, I'm not complete with you any longer; I need to join my life with this other person so I can really be complete." Your union with your spouse is complete in its potential, and you have to work to unpack the potential. You are made for your spouse *exclusively.* That's what marriage does; it keeps other people out!

And one of the first groups of people who need to be kept out of the marriage is the parents. The role of parents and extended family changes dramatically when their children marry—or it *should* change dramatically. But often there is a lack of understanding about how this shift in roles takes place. It's significant that God, while he chooses to say relatively little about the details of marriage, uses the seminal verse from Genesis to charge the husband to leave mom and dad in order to join himself to his wife.

This passage, Genesis 2:24, is the first mention of marriage in the Bible and, as such, warrants special attention. God wants to lay a foundational mind-set about marriage right from the beginning. This mind-set involves a new couple separating emotionally from their parents—and separating in a unique way from the husband's parents. This is a big enough issue that we'll take two entire chapters to address it.

The partnership between husband and wife is essential, and it must be protected from the forces and relationships that would compete against it. God says, "Don't you let it happen! You must protect the exclusiveness of your partnership against all comers." It's not just parents that can compete with your partnership; it's also close friends, work responsibilities, hobbies, and even ministry. All of these can undermine the priority you need to place on your partner. Your marriage is sacred and must be set apart, free from the entanglements of other soul ties or loyalties that can compromise the integrity of your union.

A WORK OF ART

The question remains: how do you find God's intention for the unique shape of your marriage? Do you look to your parents, one another, Scripture? Do you find the unique shape in generational currents, from your intuition, or from God himself? The answer is yes. God intends to paint a brand-new masterpiece showing his idea of intimacy, oneness, partnership, and destiny. And he wants to display this masterpiece in your marriage. He will use the same palette of colors he has always used, drawn from his unchanging character as revealed in the Bible, but every stroke will be custom-fit to your unique blend of personality and calling. And it will be beautiful!

God will draw upon themes and examples you have inherited from your parents. There is a good and right sense of multigenerational continuity that reflects his glory. God will also use brush strokes that are consistent with his intention for the current generation. Where the yearnings of this generation amplify the heart of God, they will show up in your relationship. What kind of generational yearnings? The cry for authenticity, the hunger for real community, the passion for a rich personal experience, and the intuitive reach for an artful approach to both relationship and worship. These are some of today's cultural currents that resonate with—and in fact emanate from—the heart of God. Certain men and women from prior generations modeled similar passions, but now it's going to mark an entire generation!

And, not least, God will allow each of you the fearsome privilege of holding the brush and painting what you dream into your partner. You will mirror God's heart to one another. Even as the Holy Spirit channeled divine thought through the colorful personalities and language of the biblical writers, so the Spirit will direct his wisdom to you and allow it to be colored and applied through your hands to each other. The result will be a new living testament, if you will, to the radiant beauty of God.

QUESTIONS FOR PRAYER AND CONVERSATION

1. Do you and your spouse consistently make decisions together? Do you ever find yourself caught in patterns of "nondecision"? If so, what is a recent example?

2. Is *partnership* a good description of your marriage? Why or why not? What does partnership in marriage mean to you?

3. As a couple, where are you in the process of discovering your joint destiny?

Peace of the Heart

Once empty, aching
A peace of the heart misplaced
Once cautious, taking
Care not to waste
The time

Then thrilled, rejoicing
A peace of the heart replaced
Then joy, delighting
In newness, the taste
Sublime

Now content, resting
That peace of the heart retraced
Now one, nesting
Our love, your heart placed
In mine[2]

BREAKING OUT

The Obedience of Leaving Your Parents

FIVE YEARS INTO OUR MARRIAGE we came to a crisis as a result of a bizarre occurrence. Jerome was at an afternoon meeting at the church when I (Kellie) came by to drop something off. After getting the baby buckled into the car seat, I started the engine to get the air conditioning going. Then I went around to situate our two-year-old in her car seat. But as I closed the car door, someone hit the wrong button, and all the doors suddenly locked.

So now the kids were locked inside the car, and the motor was running with the keys in the ignition. I pulled Jerome out of the meeting as I fought to control my rising hysteria. He tried to remain calm as we both attempted, unsuccessfully, to convince our two-year-old to push the unlock button…while the baby wailed. Eventually it took both a police officer and someone from the Ford dealership before the door could be forced open.

The kids were fine, but the trauma of my children being trapped where I couldn't reach them lanced the boil of my overheated tensions. In strange ways, this scenario encapsulated my feelings of isolation and alienation, and a cauldron of feelings boiled up. I felt like I was the child trapped in the car and Jerome wasn't able to reach me. Sometimes I wasn't even sure he was trying. I knew intuitively that in the battle of life, he was not on my side.

The stress overflowed that evening into a no-holds-barred fight. Jerome complained that I wasn't behind him and didn't support him, that I was disinterested in his work and wrapped up in my own needs. He felt there was no way he could win. And he told me as much.

"Well, what about me?" I fired back. "Aren't you called to be a husband and a father? I feel like a single mom! And why do you always choose your parents over me? Didn't God say that the man is supposed to leave his parents and cleave to his wife? You've never left them! And until you do, I'll never be first in your heart."

He was stunned. The weight of that truth buried him under a mixture of horror and guilt. We both grew quiet as we let the words hang in the air.

"You're right," he said quietly. "I never did leave—not physically, not emotionally, not even spiritually. I still feel this compulsion to please them in everything. What have I done?" Hot tears stained his face. As I watched his heart break, my own heart softened. Into the night we prayed and cried. And although it would take years to complete, a healing began that evening.

Making the Leap

[Kellie] Because we're talking about the "leaving and cleaving" dynamic, we have to go back to Genesis 2:24 (MSG)—"a man

26

leaves his father and mother and embraces his wife. They become one flesh." The King James translation uses the older word *cleave,* not in the sense of "to separate," as in a meat cleaver, but to hold on to something for dear life, as in "the sword cleaves to his hand." "Therefore shall a man leave his father and his mother, and shall cleave unto his wife: and they shall be one flesh."

[Jerome] God's intention for a man and a woman who possess an exclusive, loving commitment to each other is that they become one; two separate lives are merged into one new, shared reality. While they will always remain individuals, they commit themselves to a single mission, jointly owned and jointly empowered. So far, so good. This truth is repeated in thousands of wedding ceremonies every June. But it generally stops there. Scant attention is paid to the crucial qualifier: the partnership that God calls men and women to *depends upon a leaving.*

The embracing can't take place without the leaving! Why do so many people miss that truth? People prepare to build a life together, to come into that embracing kind of relationship, yet there is almost no teaching and no real grappling with what it means to leave your parents. I think couples assume that a geographical leaving—from one house to another—is all that's needed. But moving to your own place doesn't address the larger issue.

[Kellie] It doesn't get at the need to leave emotionally. It's interesting that this failure to leave tends to happen in *Christian* homes, where the mother and father have done a better job than most in training their children, in teaching them biblical truths, and in nurturing a close family life. The emotional bonding is so important and good, but sometimes when their children get married, they don't let go emotionally.

[Jerome] I think this is a bigger issue for today's young people than it was for previous generations. As my father reminded me, leaving wasn't so difficult for men and women in the past, when society expected more independence. But today, young adults are waiting much longer to get married, and frequently they move back in with their parents after college. Sociologists are coining new terms to describe the phenomenon: twixters, thresholders, kidults. Whatever you call it, there is much more opportunity today to remain physically and emotionally attached to your parents.

It's right for parents to spend the early years drawing their children in—loving them, teaching them, laying the boundaries, and cultivating an emotional identity as a family. But in the early teenage years, parents need to initiate a shift to help their children make age-appropriate decisions on their own and to cultivate the discovery of their own destiny in life. When that happens, by the time the kids are eighteen or so, they are equipped to navigate life on their own. There has to be that shift where parents begin to release their kids, bless them, and send them out.

[Kellie] Right. I call that dynamic "becoming friends." The relationship transitions into more of a friendship where parents encourage their teenagers instead of micromanaging their lives. A parent might say, "These would be good decisions for you to make" or "This is my perspective on the situation. What do you think you should do?"

A wise parent will encourage older teenagers to look to God for direction rather than to seek direction primarily from the parent. It's a shift in the foundational reality of the relationship, all in preparation to release the children into marriage. And even before marriage, the goal is for teenagers to become healthy, emotionally independent adults.

[Jerome] When God finally got through to me about the necessity of leaving and cleaving, I became angry with my parents. *How could they have allowed this to happen?* I wondered. But in the final analysis, it wasn't anyone's fault but mine. The leaving command is directed to the husband: "You leave! It doesn't matter what anyone else does or says; you have the authority, and you have the responsibility to make this fundamental shift."

But that doesn't mean it will come without cost. You might be in the family business with a company truck that reads Smith and Son. If you leave, you might have to form your own company. But you can still leave. There is no other human expectation or obligation that exceeds your commitment to your spouse! You always have the choice to do the right thing.

The Challenge of Leaving

Rick and Lisa live in the same town as Rick's parents...and have since they married four years ago. His parents love God and love them. In fact, his mom can't keep her hands off their two-year-old daughter. She drops by at least once a week to visit. Unfortunately, though, she doesn't always call first.

Whenever her mother-in-law walks in the door, Lisa gets the feeling that she is taking over. Rick's mom usually ignores Lisa and communicates with Rick. The slights aren't obvious, but they are continuous. There is the implicit disapproval of Rick and Lisa's decisions, the way they keep house,

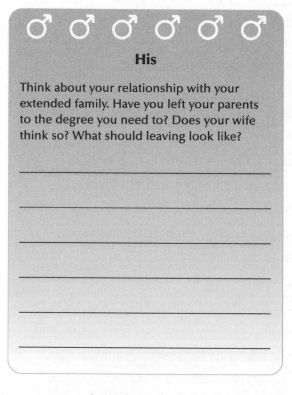

Think about your relationship with your extended family. Have you left your parents to the degree you need to? Does your wife think so? What should leaving look like?

_____

_____

_____

_____

_____

the way they parent. For Lisa, the pain has grown into bitterness and is matched only by the guilt that comes alongside the pain. She has begun to doubt herself, thinking she must be a bad wife and mother to be angry with her mother-in-law and to resent her influence over Rick.

When God brought the unhealthy dynamic to light, Rick realized he had never transferred his primary loyalty from his parents to his wife. He knew he needed to set appropriate boundaries between his family and the extended family, and he decided to lovingly confront his mom about her attitude toward Lisa. It was not an easy decision to make, and it wasn't an easy encounter with his parents.

In fact, when Rick talked with his parents, he failed to convey both the depth of the hurt that Lisa had experienced and the strength of their conviction to make changes. Rick's mom took over the conversation, and Rick did not adequately stand up for Lisa and his marriage. Since then, they have had ongoing conversations with his parents and have had to continually reinforce the boundaries he and Lisa agreed to. As they stand their ground, Rick and Lisa are beginning to repair the damage to the trust and intimacy in their marriage.

"We have lived in a new awareness that leaving and cleaving is a day-by-day, battle-by-battle affair," Rick says. "But it is absolutely necessary for the survival of our marriage that I place my wife first and foremost, rather than keeping the peace with my parents at my wife's expense."

Rick and Lisa aren't alone. Every time we have shared God's call to cut the emotional cords with parents in order to protect the marriage, couples have come to us in tears, pouring out their stories of brokenness. Parents— it needs to be said—are not the villains! The overwhelming number of parents love their children and their children's spouses and would never knowingly intrude on their marriage. The responsibility for leaving falls to the son; it is his responsibility to lay new lines of priority to his wife that can't be compromised by any other earthly relationship.

We learned these truths by walking them out and by watching our friends struggle. I (Jerome) grew up in a wonderful Christian home and had the most tightly knit family I knew. The closeness we shared was something I cherished— and still do. It shaped me and protected me from many of the pitfalls common to teen-agers. It kept me grounded in my faith and anchored in a stable family dynamic. Remember, close family bonds are characteristic of *good* homes, not bad homes. Kids who grow up in an extremely broken home can't wait to get out of the house. Leaving is pretty much a foregone conclusion.

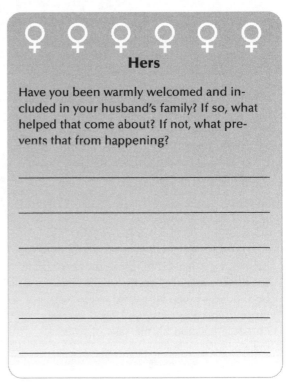

Hers

Have you been warmly welcomed and included in your husband's family? If so, what helped that come about? If not, what prevents that from happening?

_____

_____

_____

_____

_____

_____

The Best Boundaries

In determining whether you have drawn appropriate boundaries between your marriage and your parents and in-laws, consider the following questions:

1. Do you or your spouse feel violated by the frequent presence or strong influence of your parents or in-laws?

   _____

2. Do you or your spouse spend a large amount of your free time talking to or being with your parents, in-laws, or extended family, including brothers, sisters, cousins, and so forth?

   _____

3. Are most of your activities and close relationships with parents, in-laws, or extended family?

   _____

4. Do you find it hard to make major personal or marital decisions without the approval of your parents, in-laws, or extended family?

   _____

If you answered yes to even one of these questions, you need to think seriously about the appropriateness and strength of your boundaries. If you answered yes to two or more of the questions, you need to take immediate action for the sake of your marriage.[3]

In fact, kids in such homes usually leave their parents emotionally long before they leave physically.

I had the opposite experience. My home was very close. My parents did a good job of cultivating togetherness and a clear family identity. But I didn't know how to leave, to make the transition where I could be emotionally free to engage in a healthy relationship with Kellie. When I fell in love with her, even at the age of twenty-four, I was still very emotionally enmeshed with my family.

If you grew up in a Christian home, you were likely grounded in the biblical teaching that you are to honor your mother and father. We have taught our children this same truth: it's absolutely vital to respect and obey your parents.

Sons have that truth pulsing in their blood, and then they grow up and face this other commandment that says, "Leave! Leave your mother and father at the appropriate time." Men really struggle with that on a subconscious level. They don't know when or how to make the transition. How do you honor your parents and yet leave them and make your wife the priority person in your life?

Honoring your father and mother and at the same time leaving them behind so you can make your wife your priority sometimes feels impossible to navigate. It's not, of course, but when conflict arises between you and your wife, it's easy to default to your emotional wiring, which has been programmed by umpteen years of making your original family the center of your world. Godly young men enter marriage when they're still connected to their parents by an emotional umbilical cord. And because so few people emphasize the biblical requirement of leaving, this dynamic is a setup for dysfunctional and broken marriages.

A new wife comes into marriage with the reasonable assumption that she will be the center of her husband's world. She expects to be his uncontested priority, the focus of his commitment. But if he hasn't made the necessary emotional break with his parents, there will be a subtle but significant power shift back toward the parents and away from his bride. The husband has to make this fundamental realignment.

EXPRESSIONS OF HONOR

You can transfer your loyalty from your parents to your spouse while still honoring and respecting your parents. You *were* an obedient child; *now* you are a man or woman who stands first in obedient relationship to God. It's never appropriate to ridicule or shame your parents; Scripture uses harsh language regarding that kind of dishonor. But when you come into marriage, your husband or wife becomes absolutely primary, taking precedence over all other human relationships. Your spouse gets your complete loyalty and commitment. Both of our parents taught us this.

Once you are married, there is no more *obedience* toward your parents. You respect them, you honor them, you draw upon their wisdom, but there is no longer a debt of obligation to obey them. When you are married, your parents may not actually convey their will in an outright command. Instead, it may be expressed as a preference: "We would like for you to do this." But be aware that your history might lead you to interpret a preference as a command.

This is why a husband and wife, but especially the husband, need to communicate to those outside the marriage: "We are one flesh now. So *we* will make the decisions about where we will live and work and what we will name our children and whether we will go to Gramma's for Sunday dinner."

THE NECESSARY DECISION

The journey of leaving and cleaving that Kellie and I began in our fifth year of marriage progressed slowly. We began to set some boundaries around our marriage, and I attempted to make a definitive shift of priority from my parents to Kellie. It was minimally successful. Even with the weight of our newfound revelation from God, my old patterns were rooted deeply in my subconscious choices and continued to frustrate our movement toward oneness.

Four years later God again allowed us to come to a place of crisis. This time Kellie and I were attending a pastors' conference in the North Carolina foothills. I was leading worship at the conference, and since I had missed dinner, we slipped out of the teaching time to go to a nearby restaurant. Over dinner, it felt as though we were finally able to step back from our lives and take an objective look: our marriage had been compromised by years of my misplaced loyalties. And our living situation—in such proximity to my parents—had raised significant obstacles in the formative years of our marriage. My father continued to be pastor, boss, and neighbor. It wasn't his fault...but with our living in the same town I couldn't make the realignment that was needed.

Between the time Kellie and I ordered dinner and the time we paid the bill, we decided to make the biggest change we could imagine. I resigned my position on the church staff, rented out our house, and moved our family sixteen hundred miles across the country—all within three months. Because it was such a radical decision, we sought the counsel of friends, a pastor and his wife, who opened their hearts to us and strongly encouraged us to act on our intentions. It was a biggie, but we had spent too long trying to patch our hemorrhaging marriage with a band-aid; it was time for radical surgery.

We spent the next year as a sabbatical in the mountains of Colorado where we reopened all our old, festering wounds, let Jesus come in and doctor our souls, and began the process of healing in earnest. Before we could get on with life and ministry, we had to repair the damage in our bruised marriage, reconnect with God, and obtain fresh vision for our future as a family. After nine years of marriage, leaving was difficult. But hope was alive.

Many times I found myself mumbling under my breath, "If only we had done our leaving when we first got married!" It would have been so much easier on everyone concerned. As it was, our leaving was more of a tearing. Leaving was never meant to be so violent; it's meant to be an easy shift.

Our mending has come progressively over the years. My parents have consistently reached for healing as we have worked to bring the necessary realignment to these important family relationships. There are few things that God desires to do more than to bring healing to families. Most importantly, God has fully restored the trust and intimacy of our marriage.

Questions for Prayer and Conversation

1. Would you say your parents did a good job of releasing you into adulthood? Why or why not? Did you do a good job of releasing them?

2. Do you still feel pressured to conform to your parents' expectations? If so, do you give in to that pressure? In what ways?

3. Do you struggle with the tension between "honoring" and "obeying" your parents? If so, how does the struggle show itself in your life and your marriage?

Breaking In

Finding Your Place in the Extended Family

IN THE MOVIE *The Sisterhood of the Traveling Pants,* Carmen is a teenager visiting her divorced father for the summer. They have not spent time together since she was a child, and now he is building a new family of his own. It's an awkward position for Carmen, to say the least. She finds herself sitting at the dinner table with her father, her father's fiancée, and the fiancée's two teenage children. The camera pans between Carmen, who is sitting silently, and the rest of the family, who are laughing at jokes and telling stories she knows nothing about. No one looks at her or asks her questions; no one invites her into the family flow. Their shared history painfully excludes Carmen from the conversation. And from their hearts.

A similar if more subtle variation plays out in many homes today, resulting not from divorce but from a new marriage. An adult child gets married, and his or her family carries on the time-honored traditions without graciously inviting a new son or daughter—their child's spouse—into the family. Such behavior is rarely deliberate, which points out the need for married children and their parents to pursue this vital connection with wisdom and intentionality.

NAVIGATING FAMILY DYNAMICS

There's a lot of catch-up to do when a new son-in-law or daughter-in-law enters the family. Every family has its timeworn ruts—conversations and stories and jokes and family history that the new spouse has no clue to. Both the husband and the wife want to get introduced to family history on the other side, to learn about the people and the forces that shaped the person they just married.

But when either spouse's family fails to bring the new "son" or "daughter" up to speed by sharing the family's backstory, the new in-law feels excluded. If the family doesn't interpret its history but just runs along on the old tracks, the conversation flows *around* the new spouse, not *through* them. It marginalizes them.

Our identities are formed partly by our past experiences. The husband and wife start sharing their past with each other as they get to know each other. And they continue this self-disclosure throughout their marriage. Ideally, both families will want to know as much about the new spouse as they can. And they can do that by asking questions and being intentional about discovering who the new in-law is as a person. And the new son- or daughter-in-law can be intentional in the same way, by sharing his or her past with the spouse's family.

The husband also needs to purposefully incorporate his new bride into his family. And this is a new paradigm for him. Before marriage, he was responsible only for his own life. But now he has become an "us" and needs to bridge the gap to help incorporate his new bride into his family. This requires a new mind-set…where he steps into his wife's skin, so to speak, and hears things through her ears. When that happens, he can spot when she is being left out or left behind.

The husband, uniquely, needs to take on a whole new point of view where he doesn't see himself fundamentally as a son but as a husband. When he and his wife go to his parents' house, he can't fall into the old patterns he grew accustomed to as a child. And it's important to keep in mind that these same forces can operate within the wife's family. There can be attachments, enmeshments, and unhealthy emotional connections between a wife and her parents, just as they can exist between the husband and his family. Both spouses need to be intentional about finding their emotional identities in the relationship with their mate and not with their family.

FORGING NEW BONDS

One pattern that can become a real trap in new marriages is when a spouse becomes the go-between, the translator between the other spouse and the parents. Of course, it always begins that way: the woman introduces her boyfriend to her parents; the guy introduces his girlfriend to his parents. The parents want to know all about their prospective son- or daughter-in-law, and they get that picture in large part through the eyes of their child.

But once the couple gets married, there is a tendency for the earlier pattern to remain…for the husband to interpret his wife to his parents and them to her. The same dynamic holds true for the wife continuing to serve as the go-between for her husband and her parents. "No, I don't think my folks intended any offense. What they really meant was…" "No, Mom, he's not rejecting you because he has to work this weekend. He would *love* to come to the family picnic if he could."

It shows up in many subtle ways. When the phone rings and caller ID says it's her parents, he passes the phone to her instead of answering it himself. When the parents want to invite the couple for Thanksgiving, they seek out their son to talk through the plans instead of their daughter-in-law. On one level, this is understandable. It often takes a conscious effort to rechannel the relational flow from "her," in which the new daughter-in-law is a guest, to "us," in which she is a full-fledged member of the family. What helps is to be intentional about building the new in-law relationship. Husbands, take the initiative to call and interact with your wife's parents. Wives, take the opportunity to answer the phone when your in-laws call. Take advantage of opportunities to ask good questions and to interact with them in a variety of ways.

One of the best things Kellie's parents have done is to refer to me as their son. When we are all together as a family, and they introduce their in-laws to their friends, they introduce us all as their sons and daughters. They also want us to call them mom and dad. That was awkward for me initially; I think subconsciously I felt as if I was betraying the unique relationship I had with my parents. But over time it reinforced their acceptance of

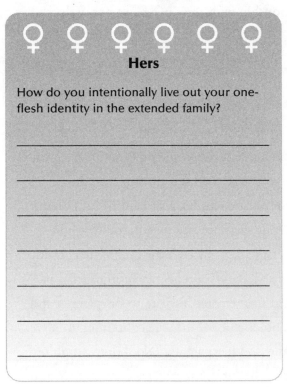

Hers

How do you intentionally live out your one-flesh identity in the extended family?

_____

_____

_____

_____

_____

_____

_____

me into their family, and that has become a great thing—something we want to extend to our eventual sons- and daughters-in-law!

FALLING FAR

When a wife fails to switch her allegiance from her family to her husband, it's just as destructive to the emerging marital relationship as when her husband makes the same mistake. But in the book of Genesis, God focuses on the husband's leaving—even though Adam didn't have any parents to leave!—in anticipation of how sin would affect marriages in the future. Someone has said that you'll never know how far we fell in the Garden until you try to go back! There are certain effects that sin will potentially have on the husband-wife relationship, effects that God wants to preclude by directing the husband, particularly, to leave his parents.

First, God is determined to preserve the equality of value between the two partners. He knew that as a result of the Fall, wives would forsake their dependency on God and would "desire" their husbands. In other words, they would attempt to use a human substitute to satisfy the divine appetite of their souls. And husbands, in their fallen condition, would take advantage of that opportunity to "rule

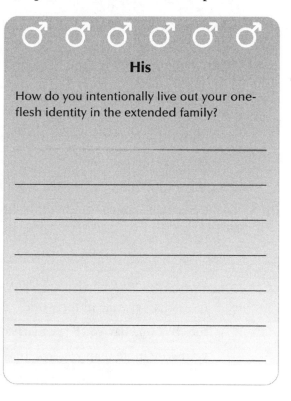

His

How do you intentionally live out your one-flesh identity in the extended family?

_____

_____

_____

_____

_____

_____

over" their wives (see Genesis 3:16). The result has been thousands of years of human history in which women have been treated as property with little or no intrinsic value. In addition, women have frequently been torn from their parents with no voluntary "leaving" on the part of their husband.

Knowing that sin would produce such inequity, God spoke this directive to all husbands: "You must leave behind your place of security and identity and craft a new and equal union with your wife" (Genesis 2:24, authors' paraphrase).

Second, God's command that husbands leave their parents addresses the unique bond between a mother and a son—a special bond that is meant to prepare a son for stepping into his destiny and a bond that also has the potential to derail his emerging identity.

THE MOTHER-SON BOND

[Kellie] As the mother of a son, I know firsthand that God made women to be nurturing and protective. Something in mothers makes them want to care for people. And with a son, a mother is drawn into that relationship differently than with a daughter. It's a unique bond.

[Jerome] Do you think it's because a son is intuitively looking to understand how to relate to his future wife by relating to his mother?

[Kellie] If it's a healthy mother-son relationship, then, yes, that can be a factor. Our son, who is eight, may say, "Mom, I love you more than anyone in the world!" And I respond, "I love you too. But one day you'll get married, and you're going to love your wife more than you love me." And he'll say, "No! I'll never love anyone more than I love you."

This is normal behavior. Little girls think they want to marry their father, and little boys want to marry their mother. But in some families a bond develops between mother and son that becomes unhealthy. The mother subconsciously feels that her son *will* always belong to her. She decides on some level that she won't give him up to anyone else. And if a mother's marriage isn't entirely healthy or satisfying, she might depend on her son's love to prop up her sense of worth.

A mother carries a God-given burden for her son. She wants her son to fulfill God's calling on his life. She prays for her son, wanting him to find his destiny. She loves and trains her little boy to become a man, and she longs for him to become everything God wants him to be. And yet a mother can hinder that very thing by not letting her son go, by not releasing him to the love and care of his wife.

The role that the mother held in the past—that of holding her son's destiny in prayer and partnership—now transfers to his wife. It's crucial that there be no competition for this role. The mother must release her place to the new woman in her son's life.

The problem of the overinvolved mother is a subtle one. She's just operating the way she always has. She's just being a mother. But she can't continue in that vein after her son is grown. It's no longer her place.

Here is the key: the mother must pass on that burden to her son's wife. The new wife now carries the vision for his life and for their new joint life.

Making this transition doesn't leave the mother out in the cold. She now has a new goal: to become her son's friend and her daughter-in-law's supporter. She has the opportunity to pursue her new "daughter" with the goal of becoming best friends, becoming her advocate and encourager. The way she can love her son best is by carving out a powerful, life-giving relationship with her new daughter-in-law.

The Gauntlet

We have friends whose story illustrates how damaging it can be for a mother to hold on to her son. David and Susan met on the Pacific coast during their first year of college and became fast friends. As they began to wonder whether God might have something more than a friendship in store for them, they started getting flak from David's parents.

"You're not ready for a relationship," they cautioned. "You need to focus on your relationship with God." But David *was* focusing on his relationship with God. He had never rebelled against his parents in any significant way, but in this instance they refused to trust his judgment. Without having met Susan, their consistent message to David was, "Break it off! God has something better for you."

David's mother in particular seemed to be motivated by fear and a desire to control her son. He had grown up under a cloud of his mother's overly careful screening of his friends, a clannish focus on their family, and his parents' refusal to let him date. His parents were committed to God and devoted to nurturing their children. Still, they harbored a constant anxiety that their kids might be corrupted, and to guard against the perceived danger, they controlled their kids' activities in the extreme. This was all David had ever known, so he never questioned it…until he met Susan.

For the first time in his life, David was torn. He would swing wildly back and forth as he thought about Susan. One week their relationship was on; the next it was off. The tension between his love for Susan and his devotion to his parents began to gnaw at his soul. During his first summer back home, he wrestled with thoughts of suicide. He desperately wanted to honor his parents, but his heart told him there was nothing wrong about his relationship with Susan. In fact, there was something very right about it!

The next year at school David and Susan decided to talk to a counselor in their church. (The counselor actually knew David's mom and dad.) As their story unfolded, the counselor pointed out that the behavior of David's mom wasn't normal or healthy. For the first time in his life, David heard that his family was seriously dysfunctional.

Over the months that followed, the counselor led David to an understanding of boundaries and individuation. "Healthy relationships require healthy boundaries," he explained, "and you need to find your own identity, not in rejecting your parents, but in separating your soul from theirs."

Changing Roles for Sons, Mothers, and Wives

With marriage, three crucial roles undergo a significant shift. Mothers who have prayed over their son's destiny for twenty years or longer now release ownership of that role. Young wives assume the role of praying for their husbands and for the destiny that they now share. And young men now look to their wives—not their mothers—for prayer support and partnership in following God's calling.

Think about your place in the transitions brought about by marriage. How has the special relationship between you and your mother, you and your husband or wife, or you and your grown son changed from what it was previously? What additional changes, if any, are needed for maximum health in light of the shifts in roles and relationships?

_____

_____

_____

_____

_____

_____

_____

Susan and David decided to invest in their relationship, but the struggles intensified. His parents issued ultimatums: "It's her or it's us!" David fell into a deep depression, and as he stood firm on his new convictions, accusations and anger flowed from his parents. That summer he decided to work overseas; it was a defining moment in his emerging manhood.

In their senior year, David asked Susan to marry him. She accepted, and he e-mailed the news to his parents. They stood firm in their objections and almost didn't come to the wedding. When they did, they made it clear they had no blessing to impart. Thus, in their first years of married life, Susan and David felt extremely awkward when it came to his mom and dad. But one crucial thing had been accomplished: David had moved his parents out of the priority position in his life. Susan's place was secure in his heart.

As they concentrated on being an "us," they laid down tight boundaries. "If you send us a package," David told his parents, "and it has only my name on it, we'll send it back!"

But redemption was waiting just around the corner. David's parents invited them to join the extended family for a week's vacation in Bermuda. On the last night of the trip, David and Susan asked his parents if they could talk. They apologized for the pain they had caused his parents—not for the decisions they had made, but for the suffering that came as a result. David's parents responded with a genuine apology for rejecting Susan. It was just a beginning, but it was the start of real healing. Over the years there have been more misunderstandings, more feelings of rejection, but the hurt has led to additional times of sharing and new levels of restoration.

Today, they still see some things differently, but there is a freedom in the atmosphere. Rarely does Susan feel rejected by her in-laws. Rarely does David feel controlled. And rarely do David's parents feel shunned. God is truly the restorer of families!

CUTTING THE UMBILICAL CORD

A few years ago we witnessed a powerful passing of roles from a groom's mother to her new daughter-in-law when we attended a friend's wedding. As part of the ceremony, both sets of parents stood by their children and prayed for them. Then the groom's mother addressed her daughter-in-law with words to this effect: "I have carried a burden and a vision for my son's life for many years now. I have prayed for him and believed that God would fulfill the calling on his life. I have nurtured him, and I have loved him. But I want to say publicly that today that ends. I pass that burden now to you. I give it to you!" It was a riveting demonstration of the emotional cords being cut. This new marriage was being released into an uncommon freedom.

Sons and mothers both need to realize that if the cord continues to entangle them after the son is married, it becomes a cord of bondage. Where before it was a cord of nurturing, it now becomes a cord of death. When they refuse to break the bond, they become life takers instead of life givers.

The Enemy's scheme—to sabotage the leaving of sons—flies under the radar of most godly men and women, most pastors, and most premarital counselors. And in the home, when men don't shift their allegiance from their parents to their wife, Satan is given free rein to advance his destructive agenda. We raise this issue not to plant suspicion or to sow division but to urge couples and their parents to evaluate their family dynamics and reach for God's best. Sons are to leave their parents; parents are to release their sons to their new wives. God's design delivers the healthiest way to love one another well.

Jesus said in characteristically succinct brilliance that love is the complete expression of God's Kingdom in the earth (see Matthew 22:36–40 and Paul's commentary in Romans 13:8–10). When you love your spouse with the intensity and longevity and integrity that God teaches, you can't help but honor your spouse…and your parents too. When you love your parents deeply and respect their appropriate place in your life, then everyone is elevated and honored.

When parents release their children and continue to love them completely, all the channels of grace are opened, and freedom is the result. The goal is not children isolated from their parents but families integrated in healthy, loving dimensions.

QUESTIONS FOR PRAYER AND CONVERSATION

1. Do you find yourself trying to interpret your spouse to your parents and your parents to your spouse? If so, how can you redirect that unhealthy dynamic?

2. How has the mother-son cord been cut in your life? Or how has it failed to be cut?

3. If you have adult children, what are the joys and obstacles of welcoming a new son or daughter into your family?

Companion of Soul

Patiently waiting for Son to thaw
A cold, dark season of soul
Earnestly praying the Spirit to bring
New light to pierce and make whole

Vigilant watchman, called alongside
You tenderly, lovingly care
For the heart of your husband, companion of soul
Your queenly qualities rare

Partners in spirit, knit into one
Blessed am I among men
That God would entrust such treasure to me
A gracious and beautiful woman

POSITIONING YOURSELVES FOR POWER

Receiving God's Authority in the Oneness of Marriage

IT WAS MONDAY, June 5. We had just finished cramming most of our earthly possessions into the largest trailer that U-Haul rented, a massive six-by-twelve-foot affair, which we attached to our trusty Ford Windstar minivan. When the last pile of stuff absolutely would not fit into the trailer, we donated it to the friends who were helping us pack. It had taken all day to load the trailer, but rather than wait for morning, we pulled out of our Durham, North Carolina, driveway that night. We were eager to put a few miles behind us and begin the sixteen-hundred-mile trek to Colorado.

First, we headed across town to drop off one of our cars at a friend's house. I was driving the minivan while Kellie followed in the little car. I turned onto the highway and accelerated slowly. Pulling this heavy trailer was going to be interesting! The sign on its fender proclaimed a maximum speed of forty-five miles per hour, and I was pondering just how closely I was going to follow that once we hit the open road. As it turned out, I never got the chance.

As dusk fell, the road was still coated with a wet gloss from an afternoon rain shower. I glanced in my side mirrors and saw no cars around me besides Kellie's. That was a good thing, because I noticed the trailer was starting to bob around. As I hit about forty miles per hour, the trailer began to shimmy. At forty-five, it lurched back and forth on the road. *This isn't going to work,* I thought. At that second the trailer yanked hard to the left, pulling its tires free from the pavement. Suddenly it jackknifed, pulling the rear wheels of my van hard to the right so that both trailer and van were skidding sideways! My heart was in my mouth.

I steered into the skid, trying to right the minivan. But we had to slide another forty feet in surreal slowness before the van and trailer aligned themselves in the same direction. "Thank you, Jesus," I breathed as I pulled, shaken, onto the shoulder of the highway. Only the mercy of God had kept other cars away from us. Kellie was, of course, as shaken as I was, having watched us hurtle out of control down the road. It was a moment before we could manage to get out of our cars.

So began our journey to Colorado.

And so began the trauma of unraveling our dysfunctional marriage. That first summer away from friends and familiar surroundings was unlike any other period of our lives. Times of silence, staring at big-sky sunsets… times of fragile, tender sharing…times of angry accusation and defense. Reading, praying, crying, struggling to understand, striving to redeem. It was the hardest and most rewarding summer of our lives. Then summer gave way to fall, at least as much fall as Colorado gets. Fall in that wild land is really just a brief pause as summer relinquishes its warm glory and winter takes a deep breath and sweeps in with triumph.

ACHIEVING CRITICAL MASS

In this chapter we want to share useful insights on how oneness affects the way authority is practiced in marriage. As we will discover, the biblical themes of oneness and authority can't be separated. Authority is a big issue, whether in life or in marriage.

Anytime you take two or more individuals and link them together in a team—a business team, a church team, a marriage team—there will be a certain amount of friction. Every person has his or her perspectives, passions, strengths, and history that rub against the perspectives, passions, strengths, and history of others in the group. People usually try to reduce the friction by creating artificial channels of authority. Such an arrangement allows some in the group to elevate their perspectives, passions, strengths, and history above the others. It doesn't have to go this way, but it often does. Occasionally, leaders arise who truly value the team and are humble enough to allow the best perspectives and ideas to rise to the top.

This level of teamwork requires one essential ingredient: genuine equality.

If team members are not convinced of both their inherent dependency on the other members and the inherent worth of the others, then the group will fail in the practice of true authority. In place of authority they will have the exercise of power. There's a critical difference between the two, although they often look the same. Power is the *ability* to make things happen; authority is the *right* to make things happen. In marriage, you need both.

Too often, marriages operate like a tension-filled committee of two in which each committee member is bent on gaining the upper hand. Instead of living in oneness, the couple lives on a battleground of power struggles, and authority is the casualty. But God designed a beautiful plan to empower couples in marriage and to release the God-given authority of marriage. Where did he do this? Once again, in the Garden of Eden.

We can't overemphasize the weight of God's declaration that "it is *not good* for the man to be alone" (Genesis 2:18). Five days of creation had heard the seal of God's approval spoken over it: "It is good." But for the first time, on day six, God's creation was insufficient—not by accident, of course, but by intention. Adam was merely part one of God's masterpiece, God's self-portrait, if you will. The beauty of God, even in reflection, was far too great for just one canvas; it required two. And the image would never be complete until the canvases were placed together in perfect unity.

You Can Find Good Help!

"It is not good for the man to be alone. I will make a helper suitable for him" (Genesis 2:18). What kind of helper did God have in mind? A personal valet? An executive secretary? A "woman Friday"? The word *helper* is pretty ambiguous until you look at the original language. What the Hebrew reveals is nothing less than stunning. *Helper* is actually a two-word phrase: *'ezer keneged.* The first word is extremely powerful. It doesn't denote the menial help that comes from a slave or a servant; it's the rescuing help that comes from an ally who is more intelligent, more capable, and more highly resourced than you are.[4] This is the "help" that Psalm 121 ascribes to God himself: "I lift up my eyes to the hills—where does my help come from? My help comes from the LORD, the Maker of heaven and earth" (verses 1–2).

This word *'ezer* is so powerful, in fact, that God had to add a second word to it in order to make it fit his intent. The second word, *keneged,* means "equal." It completes God's idea of woman being an ally, an equally empowered partner with the man in the conquest of planet Earth. Author David Hamilton says that "if God hadn't added that word *equal* to the word *'ezer,* we might have been…trying to prove that men could be leaders, too!"[5]

What emerges from God's heart in the creation of woman is—surprise!—the perfect partner for his "one flesh" mandate. There is no question that the woman is a partner worth leaving mother and father for! She is a partner who completes and complements so powerfully that Adam can confidently embark on the daunting adventure of "ruling" the earth as long as Eve is his equal partner.

The destiny that God spoke over the first couple in Genesis 1:28–30 still hangs in the air today: be fruitful, have children, bring order to the earth, rule wisely over the things I have put under your charge! This destiny was too big to have been given to one of them alone; it had to come to them both, together. And only in the oneness of equal partnership can they fulfill their calling, then as now. Only in the equal partnership of this union can *you* hear the Father say, "It is *very* good!"

The Missing Link

It is precisely in the act of becoming one in marriage that God releases his authority within the relationship. There are, of course, various understandings of how authority is meant to flow between a husband and a wife. The traditional model gives the husband the upper hand. Contemporary responses to that model occasionally reverse the hierarchy, placing the authority with the wife, particularly if she has the stronger personality of the two. But more often, contemporary models emphasize the independence of the two partners. Within this model, both the husband and the wife wield authority over their own separate lives, and they negotiate how they will manage the parts of their lives that overlap at home.

Both models generally miss the ideal that God elevates as his great desire for marriage. The familiar approaches all tend toward segmentation and separation rather than the authentic merging of two equally valued, equally resourced individuals. While the husband-as-authority model tends to empower one individual at the expense of the other, the separate-but-equal model ostensibly empowers both, but in reality it merely sets the stage for ongoing power struggles.

God's brilliance shines through these murky waters. Essentially, he says, "Until the two of you are able to recognize your inherent need for each other and you learn to fully value one another and bring your hearts into complete alignment, there will be *no authority* among you! But when you take on the humility of a servant and submit yourselves to each other, doing the hard work to hammer your different perspectives and ideas into a single, tempered vision, *then* I will release a flow of divine authority through your unity that will rock the gates of hell and advance the purposes of heaven on the earth!" This flow of authority, birthed in unity, releases righteous power through a wife and a husband in every facet of their lives. Or, we should say, in every facet of life where this beautiful union has been fought for and made their own. This is the source of authority in oneness, the design that God gave Adam and Eve when he invented marriage.

Let's consider some of the scriptures that clarify God's passion to release authority in oneness.

> How good and pleasant it is when brothers live together in unity!
> It is like precious oil poured on the head, running down on the
> beard, running down on Aaron's beard, down upon the collar of his
> robes…. For there the Lord bestows his blessing, even life forever-
> more. (Psalm 133:1–3)

There are few things as compelling and as elevating as unity among God's people. In Psalm 133, when David compared unity among like-minded partners to the anointing oil that covered Aaron's head and body, he was making a seismic statement: unity is the place of authority! The anointing of Aaron as the high priest of Israel released him into a place of unparalleled spiritual authority. And this same unity will release authority into the lives and relationship of couples everywhere.

After Jesus said this, he looked toward heaven and prayed:

"Father, the time has come. Glorify your Son, that your Son may glorify you. For you granted him *authority* over all people that he might give eternal life to all those you have given him....

"I will remain in the world no longer, but they are still in the world, and I am coming to you. Holy Father, protect them by the *power* of your name—the name you gave me—so that they *may be one* as we are one....

"My prayer is not for them alone. I pray also for those who will believe in me through their message, *that all of them may be one,* Father, just as you are in me and I am in you. May they also be in us so that the world may believe that you have sent me. I have given them the *glory* that you gave me, *that they may be one* as we are one: I in them and you in me. May they be brought to *complete unity* to let the world know that you sent me and have loved them even as you have loved me." (John 17:1–2, 11, 20–23)

The amazing prayer in John 17 was Jesus's final benediction over his friends prior to his death and resurrection, and in it he wove a scarlet thread between unity and authority. The thread looks like this: "Father, my work here is done. Thank you for giving me your authority, for I could never have brought people to you without that authority. Now I need you to equip my disciples to carry on the task of bringing people to you. They will never experience this authority unless they live in complete unity. And this won't be easy for them; they need heaven's power to find unity and to stay in it! But as you empower them with oneness, the world will see it, recognize it as miraculous, and believe in me as a result."

What a prayer! And how tragic that God's people have so rarely lived it out. Every married couple, as well as the larger community of faith, has the potential of living in the same unity and power that Jesus describes. The Holy Spirit offers us supernatural power to do what can't be done in our natural power: to live in mutual submission and true partnership. And when we do, the result is a Kingdom-advancing, world-transforming authority.

♂ ♂ ♂ ♂ ♂ ♂

His

How does your marriage reflect the "authentic merging of two equally valued, equally resourced individuals"? If you can't come up with examples that illustrate a full and equal partnership in your marriage, spend some time thinking about what that might look like.

_____

_____

_____

_____

_____

_____

Let's consider a few more examples. In Matthew 18:19 Jesus said, "If two of you on earth agree about anything you ask for, it will be done for you by my Father in heaven." His statement couldn't be clearer: the agreement of two people in prayer releases spiritual authority for God to move in power.

Luke described how the seventy-two followers whom Jesus sent out "returned with joy and said, 'Lord, even the demons submit to us in your name.' [Jesus] replied, 'I saw Satan fall like lightning from heaven. I have given you authority'" (Luke 10:17–19). Jesus had sent seventy-two of his disciples to the surrounding villages to do nothing less than what he had been doing. But to pull this off, they had to go out in groups of two. The unity that would flow through their partnership was the essential quality to release their spiritual authority.

When Kellie and I decided to leave North Carolina for a year's sabbatical in Colorado, in some sense it was the first decision of real unity we had

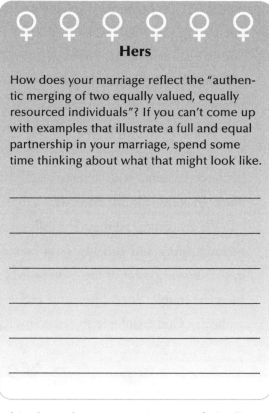

Hers

How does your marriage reflect the "authentic merging of two equally valued, equally resourced individuals"? If you can't come up with examples that illustrate a full and equal partnership in your marriage, spend some time thinking about what that might look like.

made. That act of true partnership brought an impartation of God's authority in the sphere of our oneness. Our decision was affirmed by our counselors and even confirmed by the attitude of our children. In turn, that spiritual authority (the right to make things happen) was followed by spiritual power (the ability to make things happen). God provided a house for us to rent in Colorado that absolutely defied imagination; it was the perfect setting for our unfolding sabbatical and became part of God's work of redemption in our lives. Some months later our North Carolina house miraculously sold for full price without even being put on the market! And more important, God began to release spiritual insight and power for the healing of our marriage.

We realized that more was happening than simply our working on our marriage. God began prompting me (Jerome) to write a book on some of our soul-quaking discoveries. It was the first time I had contemplated the possibility of a book. After a few months of pondering, Kellie and I came into a deep unity on the matter even though we had no natural means of getting this work published. Unity released the authority that was confirmed by a new flow of ideas, combined with the passion and ability to shape the ideas into a meaningful message. That authority brought God's power to make divine connections with strategic people who opened the door for a no-name writer to release his first book with a top-flight publishing company.

We are convinced that God calls every couple to live in oneness, which includes unity and equality. God honors that obedience by releasing his authority and power in the couple's lives and marriage. Not only does this bless the couple, but it blesses the entire world. By releasing his power and authority, God enables us to extend his Kingdom throughout planet Earth.

QUESTIONS FOR PRAYER AND CONVERSATION

1. How does authority flow through your marriage? Does that flow enhance your partnership and intimacy? Does it bless the world through each of you and jointly through your marriage?

2. How is your partner a potent ally in the adventure of life?

3. In what practical ways does your marriage express your equal worth, equal gifting, and equal partnership in life?

ROMANCING WITH GOD

Making Your Intimacy Complete

ONE MORNING I AWOKE to find the sun streaming in on a brilliant, cloudless Colorado day…and Kellie smiling at me.

"What's up?" I mumbled.

"I have something to tell you," she answered. "God did something for me last night." As the cobwebs cleared from my head, she continued. "God called me to meet with him during the night. As I was with him, he took away all my offense, and I have forgiven you. I've released my anger for all the years you didn't put me first."

As I deciphered what she was telling me, I realized this was genuine.

"God told me that if I wanted something from him, I needed to come get it. And he totally freed me from my bitterness and from the pain of the past."

Well, I thought, *this* is *good news.* I thanked Kellie from the bottom of my heart. As I did, I felt a previously unknown intimacy seeping through the cracks of our brokenness, and I reveled in the way it refreshed our souls!

A PROFOUND MYSTERY

"Intimacy with God...and one another." This has become our creed and our mission; it is the motivation behind everything we do in ministry. Appropriately enough, our Colorado sabbatical was an awakening for us in two dimensions: a call to intimacy with God and a new intimacy with each other. Time with the one you love is a natural expression of intimacy.

As we enjoyed our new revival of heart, God led us to a scripture that brings both passions together. It's found in Ephesians 5, centering around Paul's quoting the marriage mandate: "For this reason a man will leave his father and mother and be united to his wife, and the two will become one flesh," to which he adds the following commentary: "This is a profound mystery—but I am talking about Christ and the church" (verses 31–32).

"Profound mystery"? That about sums it up. And I'm not sure which is more mysterious—becoming one with your spouse or one with God! We know the former is mysterious, because we've tried it...and it doesn't come easily. And the latter is so mysterious that some people have never tried, and those who have tried aren't entirely sure what "one flesh" with God is supposed to look like. None of us really know. Yet God invites us into this mysterious journey of oneness, and there's no turning back.

Being One with God

Oneness with God, what theologians call the "divine union," has historically been the domain of Christian mystics. But it is God's deepest yearning that every one of his children enjoy complete intimacy with him. Can you believe he wants to have such a union with you? From our beginnings in Eden to the promise of heaven, God's intentions have never been clearer. In John's Revelation, he calls heaven the "wedding supper of the Lamb" (19:9). Guess who the bride is? You. God has asked for your hand in marriage. It began the day you first said yes to him, and it will culminate when you step through death's door into an eternity with him.

Jesus's love affair is with his church, of course, not just you alone. But it has very personal ramifications. Jesus "left" his Father—as all wise husbands do—in order to embrace you as the greatest passion of his heart. Part of your intimacy with him comes in the corporate worship of the community of faith, and part of it comes solo when it's just the two of you.

Being One with Your Spouse

One intimacy illumines the other. Marriage gives us the clearest glimpse into the nature of the relationship God desires to have with us. The level of exposure, trust, partnership, and ecstasy we touch in marriage is a dim but authentic shadow of the life God invites us to enjoy with him. Conversely, the depth of commitment, passion, safety, and destiny we touch in God is a heavenly hint of the potential that marriage holds on earth for every man and woman. Will you go there?

[Jerome] When we started conceiving this book, I wrestled a bit over whether to get into the topic of intimacy with God. On one level it feels a bit removed from the practical elements of marriage. But nothing else shines a light on our destined intimacy with Jesus the way marriage does. It illuminates the beauty of the partnership that God calls us to in our romance with

Jesus. Even Paul found it impossible to refrain from connecting the dots between the intimacy of marriage and intimacy
with God. (His discussion in Ephesians 5 bears this out.)
Marriage shapes our intimacy with God, and, in turn, marriage is shaped *by* our intimacy with God.

[Kellie] I have come to personally experience Jesus as the lover of my
soul. I love being married; it's something I always wanted. I
think the real beauty of marriage is that it portrays in a human
way the love that God has for us. As much as we are capable,
we try to love each other unconditionally. And that is very fulfilling. But on a deeper level, the love we experience from
God really and truly is unconditional! It comes out of who he
is as our creator, and no one will ever know us or understand
us the way God does.

I think women need to hear that, because it's so easy to look
to our husbands to fulfill the longings that we have. That's not all
bad, but it has limitations. God's love, on the other hand, is infi-
nitely satisfying. God set Adam and Eve in a perfect environment,
and he would come and walk with them in intimate fellowship.
They were completely free in that intimacy, free to be who they
truly were. There was nothing to hinder them from expressing
themselves.

MISPLACED EXPECTATIONS

Adam and Eve enjoyed complete intimacy with God and with each other,
but we know that it didn't last. When God spoke to Eve about the consequences of her disobedience, he did not curse Eve...or Adam. He only
cursed the serpent and the ground.[6] But he did speak to Adam and Eve

about the results of their sin, the impact that the curse would have on them. He told Eve that her pain in childbirth would be increased and that her desire would be for her husband, and he would rule over her (see Genesis 3:16).

The result of sin entering the world was that Eve turned away from God as her source—as the one she would rely on to meet her deepest longings and needs. Instead, she would turn to Adam to try to meet those needs. The consequence of that misplaced dependency opened the door for Adam to rule over her in a potentially oppressive way. With Eve looking to Adam to satisfy things that he was

Think About It

What are your deepest desires, and how do they rule you?

_____

_____

_____

_____

_____

_____

_____

_____

_____

_____

never designed to satisfy, it placed him in a power position where, in his fallen condition, he would dominate her.

We go after the things our hearts desire. And in the end, that desire rules us by taking over our affections. If our greatest desire is for God, he will rule us. If we most desire wealth, we'll become a slave to wealth. The same thing happened with Adam and Eve when her desire for him to fulfill her longings gave him power over her.

We see the same pattern in Adam. Instead of looking to God to satisfy his longing for deep intimacy, he looked to his work. And his work—the ground—was subjected to the curse. Instead of Adam's work being a place of partnership and fulfillment, it became a place of struggle and sweat and difficulty. We all long to return to the Garden, where work was fulfilling and a pleasure. But work is a poor substitute for the intimacy we were made to have with God.

Men continue to seek fulfillment in their work, but they also look to women to satisfy their needs. Of course, men and women are meant to fulfill certain needs for intimacy; marriage is a place of natural intimacy…an intimacy meant to mirror our relationship with God. But it can't replace that intimacy! Actually, marriage is *a conduit* for our intimacy with God.

One of the consequences of the Fall on marriage is that, instead of being grounded in intimacy with God and empowered by our partnership with each other, we are tempted to become independent of God and co-dependent on each other! One definition of codependency is two people mutually looking to the other to satisfy places in their souls that are not meant to be filled by that person…or sometimes not by a person at all, but only by God.

Another consequence of the Fall is that spouses are set up for disappointment and dissatisfaction and ultimately for anger and alienation in marriage. Their very efforts to draw close eventually result in a tearing apart when couples seek in each other the intimacy that can only be provided by God. The hope for all couples is that God will redeem the curse by anchoring spouses in intimacy with him and then source their marital intimacy from divine intimacy.

This is one reason Jesus wants us to recognize him as our heavenly lover! When you read the Song of Songs, imagine yourself in that poetic romance with Jesus. He knows you and loves you completely because of who he is. He not only created you, but he redeemed you, because you have eternal worth and value.

Women need to understand that God is not just a masculine God. God is also feminine. Both maleness and femaleness are tangible expressions of his intangible personhood. He has revealed and expressed himself in Scripture using a number of references[7] that illustrate the incredible value God places on femininity. If you are a woman, your very being is an expression of God's nature just as masculinity expresses another dimension of God.

When God created us in his image, he gave us value and worth that can never be taken from us. We are whole in God, and we don't need anyone else to confirm our worth. And yet God places people in a marriage and calls each spouse to meet the need for intimacy for the other. They become complete as they become one flesh in marriage. So the question of which needs we expect God to meet and which we expect our spouse to meet is a paradox. We need to pursue intimacy with God *and* with each other. The answer is not either/or but both/and.

Who Completes Whom?

If we are somehow incomplete in this life, then who or what serves to complete us? You don't have to be married to enjoy deep intimacy with God, nor do you have to be married to be a whole person. We need to distinguish between *whole* and *complete*—at least as we're using those words in this book. Every man and woman comes into the world broken by sin, and as we go through life, we continue to experience brokenness—brought on by our own sins as well as other people's sins against us. But God is in the business of restoring people—healing their woundedness and making them miraculously whole through Christ.

The more wholeness a man and a woman bring into their marriage, the more quickly and easily they will establish a healthy, satisfying relationship. But no matter how restored and how whole you become, you are still incomplete. You do not have all wisdom. You do not have every spiritual gift, every natural ability, every potential strength. You do, in fact, have weaknesses…and this is by design! Why? Because God intends to unwrap the wonder of completeness within—and only within—the context of community. Within partnership. It's a marvelous thing to see and a marvelous thing to live. In marriage, one partner is strong where the other is weak, and so they cover each other's weaknesses and experience the intimacy of completion as they serve each other.

And for those who are not yet married or who never marry, God does not leave them lacking. Their completeness is also found within the framework of community, within a tight-knit group of committed friends. It's sometimes more difficult to find this caliber of friendship and commitment in community than in marriage, but it is possible. And even for those who are married, God calls them into a larger community with other Christians. God invites all of us to enlarge the sphere of partnership and multiply the spiritual authority that comes with true unity.

CHANNELING THE RIVER

[Jerome] All worth comes from God, and we constantly need to be
    reminded of our true worth. My worth, objectively speaking,
    doesn't come from you or your love. But the cool thing is that
    you become a channel of God's love flowing into my soul, a
    conduit for the river of God's worth and affirmation. You
    reflect his passion and value for me in your kindness and
    encouragement.

[Kellie] We need that affirming and amplifying flow in our relationship. I need you to tell me that you love me, that you need me, that I'm valuable to you. Any intimate relationship is meant to reflect and reinforce God's heart to the other. But you don't give me worth. If you fail to communicate worth to me, I don't cease to have worth.

[Jerome] And I'm not the only conduit for God to communicate those things to you. You're in intimate relationship with God directly, and you receive his love firsthand. But in marriage we become God's partners—there's the *p* word again—to add our blessing and agreement to the things that originate in God's heart.

We all have blind spots, and in the places where we can't see clearly, we're unable to receive the things God has for us...until someone else shines a light on it. Since you have a different set of gifts and perspectives, you're able to see and illuminate both the obstacles to and opportunities for my receiving from God. You become God's spokeswoman, the tangible expression of God in my life.

[Kellie] When we view each other as our best friend and lover, we want to spend time with each other. We want to listen and learn each other's heart better. And this is the same passion that drives our intimacy with God.

Putting Feet to Intimacy

When we moved to Colorado, we knew we needed more space in our lives to pursue our intimacy with Jesus. So we created the necessary space. For that sabbatical year, we had more freedom than usual to pursue him, because we weren't working traditional jobs. Each of us took a full day

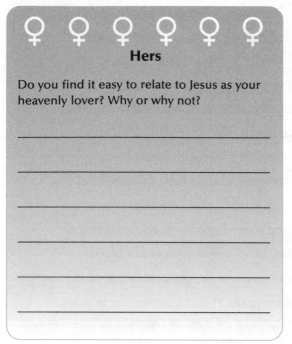

Hers

Do you find it easy to relate to Jesus as your heavenly lover? Why or why not?

_____

_____

_____

_____

_____

_____

every week just to be with God and listen to his heart.

It's not as hard as it sounds. And it isn't just on your knees praying the whole day. It's simply *being* with him…like being with a friend or your spouse. It can involve reading or journaling or even taking a nap! It can be resting in his presence. It can be singing, walking—whatever. It's saying, "God, you're my friend, and I want to know you and be with you and talk with you and experience you fully this day." God wants to be pursued; we don't always realize that about him. He wants to be loved for who he is and not just for what he can do for us.

If you don't relate to a person out of a deep value for his or her "person-ness," out of a desire to know him or her intimately, then the alternative is to *use* that person. Sometimes we end up using God, relying on him for an emotional fix on Sundays or going to him as a place of appeal when we're in trouble. This is a mockery of the intimacy he calls us to. Relying on God for help when it's convenient or we're desperate is a mere shadow of our capacity and destiny for partnership with him.

And the same is true in marriage. The goal in intimacy is not to use your spouse to gratify your needs. Intimacy involves coming into a mutual serving partnership.

But how do you pursue deep intimacy with God when life crowds in?

When we came back to North Carolina to start oneFlesh Ministries,[8] we had to acknowledge that our pace of life had increased. We didn't have the same level of space that we had enjoyed in Colorado. So how could we maintain that spiritual connection when we were devoting so many hours to launching a ministry? Part of the solution is making intimacy with God not just a good idea or a goal but a way of life.

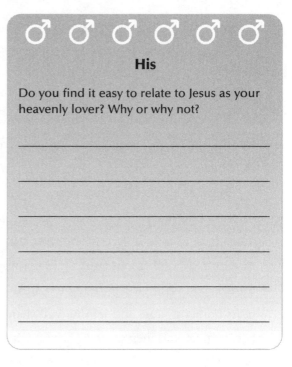

His

Do you find it easy to relate to Jesus as your heavenly lover? Why or why not?

In our marriage we would never want to live without one another. We would never choose that; the absence would leave an enormous hole. The same is true of our relationship with God. We can't live without him. Just to function in life and to be our true selves requires a certain quality of intimacy with God. It's necessary for life.

The Prayer Connection

Husbands and wives merge the intimacy of marriage with their spiritual intimacy when they pray together. The oneness that comes with being married and the unity you pursue in marriage bring the blessing of God's authority into your lives. As you pursue oneness together and seek greater oneness with God, prayer is an intimate act that brings you closer to each other and to God.

When we were first married, I (Kellie) got a real taste of the power that was released by our prayers. Jerome was new on the church staff, and we decided to pray through the church directory, praying for five or ten people a day who were in the congregation. A couple of weeks went by, and people began to tell us they knew we were praying for them. They could feel the effects of our prayers! That really opened my eyes to the power of our united prayers.

Now, at least four or five times a week, we sit face to face in our bedroom to pray together. (This is something Jerome's parents modeled for us. They have a special place where they pray every morning.) We share our thoughts. We talk about stuff that's coming up. We talk about what we're reading and what God is saying to us. At times I share something that has been bothering me, and Jerome will share a bit of wisdom or give me his perspective. And then we pray. We pray for each other, for our children, for our challenges and circumstances, and for other people. It's a vital time for us to connect with each other and with God as a couple.

It's amazing what God does during those times, the revelations that come. And the more we do it, the more addicted to it we get! It's so great. If we go a couple of days without it, when we're traveling, for instance, I start craving it! It's really a lifeline for our intimacy with each other and the avenue for our spiritual authority.

QUESTIONS FOR PRAYER AND CONVERSATION

1. One consequence of the Fall is that we tend toward independence from God and codependence on our spouse. How have you experienced the impact of the Fall in this regard?

2. When do you experience your greatest intimacy with Jesus?

3. What practices deepen your shared spiritual intimacy with your spouse?

Faithful Friend

Nine years of memories, some tarnished, some bright
Are wrapped inside history now passed from our sight
Quiet smiles and anxious tears conspire to send
My thoughts to you, woman of faith and faithful friend

Nine years of happiness, some bitter, some sweet
Transfix me with your steadfastness, a diamond born in heat
Times of testing, Gently sent, can never hope to rend
My mind from you, woman of faith and faithful friend

Nine years of earnestness, some failures, some success
Feed deep fires of tenderness and strengthen will to bless
The trust you have in me; and hope that rides the wind
Sustains my soul, woman of faith and faithful friend

FIGURING OUT WHO YOU ARE
AND HOW YOU FIT

"I DON'T DO DISHES!"

Rethinking Roles at Home, at Church, and at Work

MAYBE IT FELT THIS WAY when Christopher Columbus first heard the words "Land ho!" His heart must have lurched with wonder as he laid eyes on that new world—everything so foreign and exotic, dangerous and thrilling. For Kellie and me, the unexplored "new world" was in Colorado, a high mountain pass into undiscovered regions of the soul.

The partnership and intimacy that emerged in our marriage could not have developed so quickly, possibly not at all, had it not been for the intensity and proximity of our togetherness in this sabbatical setting. We had no book or mentor leading us into this new world; we simply knew we were being beckoned by an inner hunger, pushed by the urgency of our history, and coached by the Holy Spirit. As we moved forward into the unknown,

God deconstructed nine years of faulty assumptions and deeply ingrained patterns of behavior. And our destiny began to take form in front of us.

As we occupied the same house all day, every day, our intimacy was reshaped, and our partnership took on a tangible form. In between the spiritual disciplines of prayer, study, and writing, I (Jerome) was available for sharing daily tasks of helping the kids with their baths, cleaning the house, and running the carpool. I gained new and deeper insights into Kellie's world…and the partnership drew out of us both a new appreciation for living life together.

As Kellie was making dinner one night—she loves to cook—she asked me to grab something out of the pantry. As I fished around for the needed item, I realized there was little rhyme or reason to where cans and bags of food were located. As I ribbed her about it, she shot back a challenge: "Okay, then, you organize it!" So I did. All the grains in one spot, canned goods in another, condiments, paper products, and so forth, each in their place.

We continued to work together like never before, and Kellie mentioned in passing that she hated to shop for groceries. *That's strange,* I thought. *I love to shop for food.* "Hey," I said, "I'll do the grocery shopping if you'll do the filing." As long as I can remember, I've created stacks of bills, stacks of bank statements, stacks of receipts and warranty information… but I rarely get them into my files. So we agreed to trade duties.

Within a couple of weeks, I had charted the layout of our favorite grocery store so that I knew where everything we bought was located. Using an Excel spreadsheet, I laid out every item by aisle, along with the quantity that Kellie wanted to keep on hand. When we started running low on something, I'd do a quick inventory of the pantry, make the shopping list, and hit the store. I wasn't fast, but I was thorough! On the other end, Kellie talked me through all my piles of documents, made labels for missing files, and got my office organized pronto. It was invigorating for us both. More important, it gave each of us ownership of the other's world and began the process of meshing those worlds into a shared domain.

CARVING YOUR OWN CHANNEL

When you talk about the practical outworkings of partnership—taking it into the home, the workplace, and the church—there aren't any hard-and-fast rules to follow. In this case that's an advantage, because we're trying to move away from such a limiting view of partnership. The Bible's few references to roles for men and women are directed toward specific situations in specific times (see 1 Timothy 2:11–15, for example). But God calls men and women to Christlike attitudes of the heart for *all* times and places.

Instead of predetermined rules that define what men and women do, we're reaching for a "partnership mentality." Marriage is an invitation into a new realm of teamwork; your one-flesh charter is a call to bring everything within the boundaries of your lives into the sphere of togetherness. Over the course of years you'll work out the tangible expressions of your equality and discover the practical applications of partnership.

Allow yourself to be stretched by this concept of a partnership mentality. It's easy to say, "Yeah, I believe we're partners." But if you look at how you live day to day, you might find you are traveling down preestablished ruts that you inherited from the society around you, ruts that create an inner dissonance. Without realizing it, you can fall into a superimposed way of thinking...or, rather, of *not* thinking!

Couples need to understand that God blesses them with choices. You have tremendous freedom to live life the way God wants to express himself through you. You have options. Living in partnership is a matter of choice.

SCRUBBING YOUR HEAD

The idea of living in a new way as a married couple makes me (Jerome) think of repentance. Entering the Kingdom of God is fundamentally about having a change of mind. Part of our redemption is having God scrub from our heads all the stuff we accept without careful analysis or understanding! It's really important for a couple moving toward marriage to clear the table of all their preconceived ideas. Begin the process by saying, "What does God say about this?" and "Who are we?" And then ask, "What is God saying to us? What does that mean for our lives, independent from everything we've observed or assumed?"

A helpful way to do this is to move away from your families for a year or two immediately after marrying. Go to a place where you've not been before—a location that is totally new to both of you—and start a life together. By doing that, you are forced to depend on each other (and God, of course)! The togetherness you establish in this early season will become the foundation of your relationship in the years to come. We experienced this after nine years of marriage…and by that time, we had much to recover from. But it really saved us.

One pastor of a megachurch teaches young couples what he calls "the thousand-mile, two-year rule." He urges every newly married couple to move at least a thousand miles away from their families for at least two years. That's bold and probably ruffles some feathers, but he's right on target.

Once your marriage is established on its own terms, free from the gravitational forces of family, you are free to return if you wish. You have earned your freedom by choosing each other and placing each other first in your life. For us, it was important after our time away to come back to North Carolina and rear our children where their lives could be shaped and influenced by their grandparents, aunts and uncles, and cousins. And where we could renew the vital connections with extended family.

Putting distance between you and your extended family is all about looking at who you are, examining your past assumptions, and then searching out what God has called you to. It looks simple when you put it on paper, but it's a process that takes time and discernment. Sometimes you'll find yourselves in a waiting season,[9] listening for God to reveal his purposes or his timing. Then, as God reveals his destiny for you, you have to grapple with important questions: Who will be the breadwinner in your home? Will you both work, especially before you have children? Maybe you'll decide that you each want to work part-time...and then use the extra time together to develop your relationship or minister in the church or do volunteer work or invest your lives in some other thing.

Perhaps the wife is established in a career, and she will become the family's primary financial support. You need to look at who you are as individuals—your separate strengths and weaknesses, your likes and dislikes, your goals and passions. We know that men and women are fundamentally different. Women have more nurturing and relational tendencies than men, as a rule. Men are frequently more goal oriented, more bent toward accomplishing and conquering.

But that doesn't hold true for every man or every woman. There are husbands who enjoy working in the home, who are particularly good with children, and who thrive in the kitchen. There are wives who prefer to be in the work force and who have greater earning potential than their husbands. Just because it's a nontraditional role doesn't mean it's a nonbiblical role.

A Mutual Domain

[Kellie] I sometimes hear the word *domain* used in relation to the
home. I don't think God has established individual domains
in the home—a "his" domain that includes yard work, repair-
ing the car, and unclogging the toilet, and a "hers" domain
that involves taking the kids to the doctor, shopping for groceries, and cooking and cleaning. Some people extend the idea
of respective domains into the outside world as well. But it's
equally misleading to think that the wife's domain is the home
and the husband's domain is the workplace. Those kinds of
role definitions tend toward separation rather than oneness.

And beyond that, the idea of separate domains communicates
that your assigned role is who you are: "I'm a cook and home-
maker" or "I'm a mechanic" or "I'm a stockbroker." We are condi-
tioned to find our identity and worth in our respective roles, but
that is so contrary to who we are in Christ and who we are as
partners in a marriage. Even if you follow what modern society
considers to be traditional roles, with the husband at work and
the wife in the home, the home is not "her domain." It's "*our*
domain"! And even a husband's or a wife's workplace is the
couple's shared domain.

For example, if both spouses are working outside the home,
they need to be accessible during the day by phone or e-mail. It's
important for you to know the people at your partner's workplace
and to be familiar with the projects your spouse is working on.
In marriage, you are one; you can't fulfill your vision and calling
alone. Each spouse has wisdom to offer the other in the difficult
situations he or she will encounter at work.

[Jerome] Even if one spouse is in a technical field, relational issues are usually more important than the technical ones, and the other spouse—with the advantage of emotional distance—may have greater discernment on these relational issues.

[Kellie] And in marriages in which one spouse remains at home, the spouse who is working outside the home needs to be even more accessible. There may be a discipline problem or some other issue with the kids, and the spouses need to have a partnership mentality toward all of life. Both partners need to know what's going on in the other's world—the struggles, challenges, and triumphs.

Partnership is never more essential than at the end of a workday. When one of you comes home from an outside job, it's not as though you have just worked eight hours and are now "off." Maybe you will make dinner. Or one of you might take the kids so the other can have a night out with friends. Partnership is a means of serving one another 24/7.

Modern American culture has corrected some of the more egregious inequities between men and women so that young couples may not realize just how disparate and narrowly defined marital roles were only a few decades ago. A widely circulated article titled "The Good Wife's Guide" highlights eighteen ways for a good wife to welcome her husband home from work. This article supposedly appeared in 1955 in *Housekeeping Monthly* and may in fact be bogus. But it nonetheless reflects a mentality that was alive and well in the postwar era.

Many of the suggestions were kind and gracious gestures that anyone would appreciate receiving as a welcome, but the author went beyond those with commentary that uncovers a stunning gender bias. Consider these statements: "Let him talk first—remember, his topics of conversation are more important than yours" and "Don't...question his judgment or integrity. Remember, he is the master of the house and as such will always exercise his will with fairness and truthfulness." After a host of entreaties to wives to cater to their husband's slightest whim and subordinate their own feelings, perspectives, and desires, the article ends with this decree: "A good wife always knows her place." And that place of value and worth, according to the article, lies well beneath her husband.[10] These deep-seated beliefs robbed untold marriages of the blessings of partnership!

Similar attitudes continue to damage marriages today, and unfortunately they are reinforced in Christian families that embrace a faulty understanding of the wife as "helper." (For more on the biblical concept of "helper," turn back to chapter 4.) Such a mind-set often places the wife in the role of simply helping her husband to succeed. If he succeeds, then she succeeds. A more balanced mind-set recognizes and promotes mutuality: both husband and wife serve each other and assist each other to become the best they can be. Anything short of this undermines the ideal that God desires for us.

Consider the zenith of feminine virtue in the Bible, the Proverbs 31 woman. This woman combines the nurture and care of her household with an unflinching boldness in entrepreneurship. While she is compassionate, artistic, hardworking, and brings honor to her husband (traditional feminine values), she is also an astute businesswoman, taking the initiative and authority to enter into business negotiations and run an extensive, multi-industry operation. She isn't managed in her labors by her husband; in fact, while she clearly has his blessing, she remains the CEO of the business. Her ability brings not only her husband's admiration, but even the leaders of the city respect and affirm her leadership.

[Jerome] This passage sheds light on God's empowering vision for women. But in itself, even this description isn't complete. I think God is continuing to unveil his passion for partnership by inviting men and women beyond "separate but equal" into "united and equal." Think how powerful it would be for the Proverbs 31 woman to be joined by her husband, where both her business and his are jointly managed. While the culture of that time may not have allowed such freedom, today's culture surely does. More important, God's culture relishes such expression of partnership.

[Kellie] If a Christian woman excels in the marketplace, she runs the risk of being criticized by certain segments of the church. If she excels in the home, she may be criticized by certain elements of the broader culture. Homemakers, particularly, continue to be undervalued and dismissed in the world. The church, though it still tends to accentuate the different roles of wives and husbands, has done a good job of elevating the virtue of motherhood and the value of home and family life.

[Jerome] The church has raised up homemaking as a worthy endeavor. But to assign home life to the domain of the woman—and not to husbands and wives as partners—is just one more form of undermining their one-flesh destiny. Both home and business enterprise, as intimated in the rulership mandate of Genesis 1:28, are given as a joint possession and a joint commission to the man and woman.

The Freedom of Flexibility

[Kellie] There are seasons in life when one spouse might have extra
commitments and time demands. Getting a graduate degree
or training for a different career or raising young children
makes it hard for a couple to do all that their hearts desire. So
during a certain season, they might focus on the husband's
career, and later they can shift and focus on the kids or on the
wife's career. There are different ways to bring a couple's joint
destiny into reality.

[Jerome] Yes, but I also want to encourage some care in using terms
like "his career" and "her career." In a technical sense that's
accurate, but a vision for partnership brings a couple to a
place where, no matter whose career is currently getting attention, it's still in a very real sense "our career." His job and her
job become various facets of their joint calling. So no matter
who or what is on the front lines right now—school, work,
children, or ministry—there is a keen sense of ownership and
vesting from *both* partners.

[Kellie] Yes. If you work to support the family so your mate can go
to grad school, you're saying, "I'm with you. I'm going to help
you meet the goals that you have, that *we* have."

[Jerome] That's true, but in a situation like that, make sure it's a *full*
partnership. The wife might be funding grad school for her
husband, making sacrifices for it and investing in other ways.
But she still might miss the experience of *really* partnering in
her spouse's schooling. That's the difference between functional
vesting and emotional vesting. When spouses bring a deep
personal involvement to their partners' further development—

86

in education, ministry, or some other realm—along with the practical support, then they are truly sharing each other's world and know what it means to be engaged as a team.

Within the corporate world, couples need to realize they have choices. If you're in a demanding setting at work, you need to contend for your personal boundaries. If your job involves travel, for instance, you may have to say that you won't travel more than a certain number of days a month. A healthy partnership in marriage sets boundaries around *all* the dynamics that affect that partnership. So keep your marriage in mind even when you're at work. If you need to take a long business trip, for example, consider taking your spouse with you.

Ideally, you grapple with these issues *before* you step into a job so that you consider your boundaries and your season in life as you select the position. With those convictions and values in front of you, you can avoid accepting a set of responsibilities that will violate your priorities. But for most of us, our priorities develop over time. Then we may have to face the reality that we are in a job that conflicts with the emerging value of partnership in our marriage. That's a place for tough decisions.

If your boss isn't willing to change your job requirements or to work with you in light of your boundaries, you may need to look for a new position. You have to consider what will promote your sacred partnership. Another option might involve taking a demotion—and a cut in pay—to a position that involves fewer hours at work and less travel. This is never easy, of course, but sometimes trade-offs are necessary to live sanely. Couples who hold to partnership values in marriage may find themselves redirecting their careers—away from corporate ladder climbing.

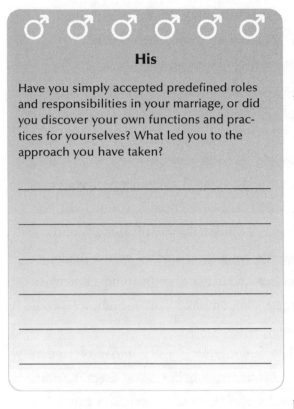

His

Have you simply accepted predefined roles and responsibilities in your marriage, or did you discover your own functions and practices for yourselves? What led you to the approach you have taken?

_____

_____

_____

_____

_____

_____

Here's another practical application of a partnership mentality. Let's say that your job requires you to go out to dinner with clients or your own work team. There's nothing wrong with that. But include your spouse when possible. (If you have to get a baby-sitter to make this work, go ahead and do it.) It's so important to integrate your worlds. It proclaims to your co-workers that you and your spouse are connected in a special way. It not only promotes partnership, but it provides a safeguard too…against someone who might want to intrude on your relationship. This applies to business travel as well: an active partnership mentality guards what is most valuable to you.

Putting on the Church Hat

We were in ministry for the first nine years of our marriage. It was our job, which raises a different set of issues compared to couples who volunteer in ministry. But either way, look for opportunities to increase your partnership in ministry. We envision ministry that values the same degree of partnering in leadership that we have been exploring in the context of the home. God doesn't ask us to segment our lives by saying, "Well, we're partners at home, but when it comes to church and ministry, you have your calling, and I have mine."

It's true that each spouse has unique gifts, but this gives couples the opportunity to blend their gifts so they can maximize their joint calling and release their spiritual authority in the church setting. It's hard to think of any function or ministry within church life that would not benefit and potentially be transformed by this level of partnership in couples.

[Kellie] We have wrestled with the fact that Jerome has a musical gifting and I don't. We have wondered how we can partner in this area, since he is often on the stage leading worship and I'm sitting in the congregation. Sometimes you have to stretch and reach for partnership in ministry when there's not a clear-cut way.

[Jerome] I can sing and play guitar…but that's not all there is to leading worship. Kellie has a unique ability to discern what God is saying and doing in a

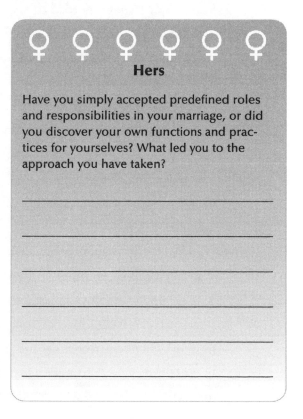

Hers

Have you simply accepted predefined roles and responsibilities in your marriage, or did you discover your own functions and practices for yourselves? What led you to the approach you have taken?

communal worship time. So we're experimenting with ways to work together to bring maximum leadership right at that point.

[Kellie] Here's an example of partnership that really worked, even though Jerome was the visible leader and I was part of the congregation. Jerome left home ahead of the kids and me one Sunday so he could get to church early. But as we were driving, I experienced a growing excitement—a Holy Spirit excitement—and I couldn't wait to see what was going to happen! I got to church a bit late, and Jerome and I didn't have a chance to talk.

Through the first couple of songs, I felt a strange sadness. I felt the Spirit say we needed to make room for something new. I knew that God wanted Jerome to stop playing the old songs and make room for whatever God wanted to do at that moment. But I didn't know what that was.

Nor did I know how to get word to Jerome up on stage. I knew in my heart this was from God, so I left the service, wrote a note on a piece of paper, and had our son, Thorpe, give the note to Jerome. When Jerome read it, he was receptive...but he wondered what it meant: "God wants to do a new thing. Stop doing the old thing."

[Jerome] I agreed with Kellie's message, but I didn't know what to do! The only thing I could think of was to back off the song we were singing and go into an extended instrumental. It created some space for what God had in mind: a wholly unexpected musical dynamic with drums and percussion. After a couple minutes it really started to connect with the people in a spiritual way—far beyond my understanding.

This led to a powerful time of worship that we had not experienced before. It opened a door for the church that lasted twenty minutes or longer. And it was exciting that God had used Kellie and me as a team! He gave the instructions to her, and she had to get them to me. If either of us had not cooperated, that powerful experience of worship would have been lost. Ever since then, we have known more than ever that Kellie should not remove herself from my worship ministry. In fact, she needs to be *more* involved with it.

There are ways to make yourself a part of your spouse's ministry even if it's not a natural part of your gifting. This is far removed from saying, "You have your gifts, and I have mine. You do your thing, and I'll do mine."

God brought you together to serve as equal partners. He has given women the freedom to be *full* partners—not just junior partners. The church benefits greatly from couples who minister in partnership. A pastor can work together with his or her spouse. The elder board (or whatever leadership structure your church follows) can consist of couples: men and women ministering in partnership.

This doesn't preclude the role of singles in church leadership, but we're focusing here on the partnership potential of married couples. In chapter 5 we talked about how God releases power and authority through unity. Unity can take place among a leadership team of just men too, but there is a higher calling and a greater potential to the unity found within the covenant of marriage. And that high potential can fuel the church as well as the home.

COLORING INSIDE THE LINES

We can't talk about partnership in ministry without discussing passages in Scripture that appear to prohibit women from leadership in the church. It's not our purpose to do an exegesis on those passages. Fortunately, there are scholars who have already done that—on both sides of the issue, of course—attempting to clarify the original meaning of those texts. After considering both sides of the argument, we have come to believe that the most authentic understanding of Scripture is found in what is usually called the egalitarian view.

God invites both men and women into roles of leadership. Each brings gifts and perspectives that are shaped by the person's femininity or masculinity, and it is in the intersection of the two that God's wisdom and nature are most clearly demonstrated. The interpretation of the pertinent biblical passages is, in our view, wonderfully unwrapped in the book *Why Not Women?* by Loren Cunningham and David Joel Hamilton with Janice Rogers. But either way you understand the scriptural injunctions, there are ways to promote partnership in leadership if you deeply desire this kind of teamwork.

But before you build partnership, you have to understand the obstacles against it.

Cunningham and Hamilton cross-reference biblical interpretation with the culture of the New Testament as they examine the plight of women throughout history. Beginning with the Greek storytellers Homer, Hesiod, and Semonides and moving on through the Greek philosophers Socrates, Plato, and Aristotle, a systematic hatred of women was unleashed upon Greek civilization. And this is the heritage that most influences our current worldview. Greek mythology, poetry, and philosophical writings portray a shocking view of women as the origin of evil and the cause of conflict and suffering. Women are portrayed as cowardly, dishonest, and innately sub-human. "That is why, wherever possible, Aristotle advised the males to be 'separate from the female, since it is something better and more divine.' No wonder homosexuality flourished in ancient Greece."[11]

When the Roman Empire conquered the Greeks, the Romans assimilated what they believed to be an intellectually superior body of philosophy, literature, and art. They adopted the same pantheon of gods and goddesses, simply rebadging them with Roman names. In this way Greek thinking spread throughout the Roman Empire, their misshapen values and fundamental mistrust of women infiltrating Roman-occupied Palestine in the first century.

Jewish culture could have retained the roots of honor and equality for women established in its heritage, but such was not the case. Abandoning its Genesis foundations, the Judaism of Jesus's time was only a dim reflection of the past, shaped primarily by the oral rabbinic traditions gathered in the Mishnah and the written teachings of the Tosefta, Jerusalem Talmud, and Babylonian Talmud. Armed with statements such as "Compared with Adam, Eve was like a monkey to a human being,"[12] the Pharisees removed women from worship, from commerce, and from education. The world Jesus entered was a very hostile and oppressive place for women.

And into that world, Jesus and later Paul moved in bold and controversial ways to elevate women to a place of safety, inclusion, and destiny. "Standing against what nearly everyone in his time believed, Paul declared the truth with echoes from the first three chapters of Genesis: Men and women have a shared origin, a shared destiny, a shared tragedy, and a shared hope."[13] This is the basis of our passion for partnership in every sphere of married life. This is the high intention of God as we understand it, and it continues to be a source of unparalleled joy, satisfaction, and effectiveness in our marriage and ministry.[14]

ENLARGING THE CIRCLE

[Jerome] There's another place in married life where partnership
shines, and that's in the realm of community. Of course,
there's the community of the church, but there is also the
sphere of relationships you have as a couple. It's common for
couples to experience a level of separation in their friendships:
she has her friends, he has his friends...

[Kellie] Which isn't a bad thing per se. It's good to have your own
friends, but you also need shared friendships. Having other
couples that we relate to mostly as a couple has greatly
enhanced the relationship dynamic for us.

[Jerome] It has opened up a new realm of communal friendship for
us—a dynamic that draws Kellie and me closer at the same
time it draws us closer to our friends. The relationships reinforce our partnership.

[Kellie] Before we were married, I had friends who were guys. It was
fun to hang out with them and get their perspective on life.
Once we got married, Jerome became my best friend. Yet we
both still need friends of the opposite gender, to get their
unique input. And when we relate to friends as a couple, we
get that type of input in a healthy, life-giving way. It enriches
our lives and theirs.

We are casting a vision for a joint ownership of life in which each partner
feels a keen sense of authority and responsibility for every facet of the big
picture. When this vision becomes a reality, both husband and wife can

honestly say, "This is *our* home, *our* kids, *our* work, *our* ministry, *our* friends, *our* community, *our* destiny." Each of you is a distinct individual, but you can join all that you are in a full partnership to do life together!

When life gets segmented into her and his responsibilities, either intentionally or by default, there is almost always inequity, either real or perceived. At some point one partner will feel that he or she is carrying an unfair share of the load. That frustration easily mutates into resentment, bringing further separation. Any arbitrary assignment of responsibility between spouses results in a *constant imbalance* in the load. The solution is partnership, a flexible "response-ability" that allows your sense of shared ownership to move each of you to respond to needs as they arise.

This doesn't prevent one partner from taking a lead in areas he or she is most passionate about or is more gifted in. If one spouse is a CPA, it probably makes sense for that person to take the lead in family finances. But if the CPA is facing deadlines at work as April 15 approaches, it might be good for the partner to balance the checkbook, pay the bills, and respond to other immediate needs.

The traditional mind-set finds one partner stressing to fulfill his or her responsibilities while the other partner looks on compassionately...or not. But that attitude can quickly degenerate to "I sure hope you get your act together and get your stuff done, because if you don't, my comfort is going to suffer." And even if there is more of a servant heart present, the attitude can be "I'm going to pitch in and help *you* take care of *your* responsibilities." Neither one reflects the full partnership that God calls us to.

The partnership mentality says, "Okay, today we have to do these things. How are we going to get them done? What is the state of each of our emotional resources and time resources, and how can we cover all the bases together?" Joint ownership brings a life-giving flexibility and connectivity that enhances the sense of teamwork in your marriage.

One caveat: this level of partnership requires a high level of trust and communication. Your established channels and habits of communication may be insufficient for this level of partnership, so you can expect to grow and stretch in this area if you choose to pursue full partnership in your marriage.

But growth involves reaching for more, and your marriage won't grow if you settle for mere maintenance. Most marriages fall somewhere between separate roles and full partnership. And to make matters more interesting, your circumstances and relationship will fluctuate from season to season. The goal isn't to justify yourself or condemn yourself. The goal is to reach for God's highest and best. To reach for the humility and servanthood that undergird biblical partnership in marriage.

QUESTIONS FOR PRAYER AND CONVERSATION

1. Does your marriage consist of separate his and hers domains, or do you concentrate on mutuality and partnership?

2. How have you learned to enhance each other's spiritual gifts and ministry through partnership?

3. How does your personal community work? Do your close friendships tend to be couple-to-couple or separate spouse-to-friend relationships?

WHO ARE YOU?

Finding Your True Identity in Marriage

IT WAS MONDAY, January 13, 2003. We had just finished signing the papers to purchase our new house. For the first time in almost three years, all of our possessions would finally reconvene under one roof, and we were some kind of ready! I (Jerome) pulled the loaded truck into our new driveway so we could carry hundreds of boxes through our new garage into new rooms in our new house. It all felt very, uh…new.

You've done it, so you know the drill. Your wife unpacks the kitchen; you do the garage. She helps the kids open their boxes while you do the really important stuff like wire up the surround sound. But let's dig a little deeper. Your differences go far beyond which rooms you tackle first. The bigger differences have to do with *how*…and *why.*

When we moved, Kellie was amazing. She was a woman on a mission! By Friday almost every box had been opened, every room set up, and—I kid you not—she had pictures on the walls. Of course, I was busy too, but in a different way. In between the required "manly" stuff (hooking up the washer and dryer and rearranging couches), I was picking out shelves to go in our study and directing landscapers where to plant cypress trees in the backyard.

Yes, I'm drawn to technical things like hooking up the CD player to the intercom, and Kellie is drawn to decorative things like bedspreads and curtains. But it's more than that. She wants things done...to get them done. I want the same things done...*so* I can enjoy the experience they'll bring us. Kellie is more goal oriented while I am more process oriented. She is more practical, and I am more creative.

Our differences pop up at odd times and in odd places: ordering dinner in a restaurant, planning a worship service, going grocery shopping, or counseling another couple. Kellie sees the root issue, discerns the goal, and seizes the moment. I want to relate, understand, and work the ideas. She enjoys beauty but is passionate about function; I value function but am passionate about beauty. She wants to conquer; I want to connect.

But wait a minute. Isn't it usually the man who wants to conquer and the woman who wants to connect? Isn't the husband usually into goals and the wife into process? Do the familiar stereotypes really fit anymore? Can broad categories even come close to accurately describing men and women today? And what about the Bible? Does God's story describe femininity and masculinity in timeless detail, or is there some latitude for individuality and uniqueness among God's creations?

So many questions. So many *different* answers!

Kellie and I discovered early on that we don't fit neatly into the conventional boxes associated with manhood and womanhood, particularly as taught within traditional church structures.

Another thing we discovered is that the same is true for many of our friends. Apparently, we're not the only oddballs around! It seems that men and women now feel the freedom to express themselves in a greater variety of ways and yet remain deeply biblical.

A third thing we discovered is that much of what has been absorbed into the church's understanding of roles for men and women finds its origin in cultural ideals of the mid-twentieth century rather than in the pages of Scripture. In other words, the evangelical understanding of masculinity and femininity may be more informed by Ward and June Cleaver than by Jesus and Paul. (In case you're not old enough, the Cleavers were the idealized family showcased in the hit television show *Leave It to Beaver*, which aired from 1957 to 1963—and seemingly forever in syndication.)

In chapter 6 we pointed out the benefits of establishing a partnership that is not shaped by predetermined roles but rather expresses itself in a series of flexible functions within the home, workplace, church, and community. If roles in marriage are not defined biblically but individually, according to each couple as they live together in oneness, then we're left with questions regarding personality types: What is characteristic of men, and what is typical of women? Does the Bible limit males to certain personality profiles and women to others? And how do your personality types shape your partnership?

Building Boxes...and Breaking Them

Personality profiling is not a new concept. The classic temperaments of sanguine, choleric, melancholy, and phlegmatic have been around for twenty-four hundred years. But the last few decades have seen an explosion of interest in and resources for understanding personality, motivation, and gifting in deeper ways. Each of the handful of personality tests we have

The Injury

We were cleaning in the basement—Kellie and I and our girls, Abigail and Ashley. Our son, Thorpe, was three at the time, and we could hear him playing upstairs. Suddenly our cleaning was halted by a long, piercing scream from the upper level. We bolted up the steps two at a time to find Thorpe lying on his back, blood flowing from his head! An upended stool in front of the closet told the story: Thorpe had stood on it, trying to reach toys high on a shelf, and had lost his balance and landed hard on the tile floor.

The swelling pool of blood stopped me dead. Sinking to my knees, I began to rub my temples and mumble, "O God…O God…O God…" I was paralyzed. The rawness of my son's trauma transformed me from responsible dad to frozen bystander.

Fortunately, the Warrior sprang into action! Kellie grabbed a towel and pressed it against the two-inch gash to slow the bleeding. "Pick him up," she commanded as she ran for the car. I held Thorpe and tried to calm him during the fifteen-minute Indy 500 ride to the Urgent Care. When life becomes threatening, you want a Warrior by your side!

taken has given us a different and helpful set of lenses to further perceive the mystery of who God created us to be. The goal isn't to push people into a defining box but rather to describe personality trends and tendencies, affirm people's wiring, and then release them to be who God made them to be!

So, as if there aren't enough already, we're going to give you a *new* profiling tool. This is not intended to compete with other approaches but to provide you with a very simple model that we developed in our journey, one that has helped us make sense of ourselves and, more important, our relationship. We discovered a fundamental divide between two types of souls: the Warrior and the Artist. You will notice dramatic differences in the areas of motivation, values, worldview, identity, strengths, and weaknesses as well as leadership and communication styles.

It's great to garner new perspectives on your personality, but it's even more important to understand how your hardwiring and your spouse's set up unique opportunities for oneness and partnership. The combination of Warrior and Artist that best describes your marriage will offer insight into the way you and your spouse tap your teamwork potential. So here's a quick quiz to get you started. It's likely that the terms *warrior* and *artist* already ring a bell, but the questions on the following pages will clarify the meaning of these personality types.

After you have circled the number that corresponds with how strongly each statement describes your personality, go back and write the number you circled for each question in a box on the right-hand side of the chart. Answers to the odd-numbered questions go in the left-column boxes; answers to the even-numbered questions go in the right-column boxes. Then add up both columns and see which side has the higher number. If your higher number lands on the left, you're an Artist; if it is on the right, you're a Warrior. The greater the difference between the two totals, the more strongly and consistently you function within your profile. The more similar your totals, the more balanced your personality is between the two.

How you're wired	Never	Rarely	Some-times	Usually	Always	Odd	Even
1. I tend to be moody.	1	2	3	4	5		
2. I handle the practical details of life with ease.	1	2	3	4	5		
3. I enjoy things that are beautiful even if they are not practical.	1	2	3	4	5		
4. I see issues in black and white.	1	2	3	4	5		
5. When something is important to me, I feel driven to communicate that passion to others.	1	2	3	4	5		
6. Injustice makes me angry.	1	2	3	4	5		
7. I have more great ideas than I could ever pursue.	1	2	3	4	5		
8. I am decisive and stable.	1	2	3	4	5		
9. I spend significant time reflecting on the meaning of events in my life.	1	2	3	4	5		
10. When something is important to me, I feel driven to make it happen.	1	2	3	4	5		

WARRIORS AND ARTISTS

Keep in mind that with any system of personality profiling, no one fits perfectly into a single category. There is some Warrior and some Artist in every

How you're wired (cont.)	Never	Rarely	Some-times	Usually	Always	Odd	Even
11. I am drawn to small groups that are centered around self-discovery.	1	2	3	4	5		
12. I tend to be critical of others.	1	2	3	4	5		
13. I enjoy expressing myself creatively.	1	2	3	4	5		
14. I am fiercely competitive.	1	2	3	4	5		
15. I tend to derive my value from the affirmation of others.	1	2	3	4	5		
16. In a conflict with someone, I have to be forceful to get my point across.	1	2	3	4	5		
17. I have a tendency to doubt myself.	1	2	3	4	5		
18. I can usually discern what motivates people's actions.	1	2	3	4	5		
19. I tend to withdraw in times of conflict.	1	2	3	4	5		
20. I am naturally good at solving problems.	1	2	3	4	5		
Totals							

human soul. Plus, there are circumstances and settings that rightly require every man and woman to go to war for something precious or, alternately, to create something artistic. But underneath what you do lies who you are, your deeper identity. And that's what we're after here. Do you engage the world and your partner from a soul that's wired primarily as a Warrior or an Artist? The answer to that question will affect how you build a life-giving union and pursue a world-changing destiny.

The Warrior

Let's begin with the Warrior. First, being a Warrior does not automatically mean you are a man. Although physical warfare throughout history has leaned heavily toward men, when it comes to the Warrior *soul*, a large slice

The Photographer

When I (Jerome) was a sophomore in college, my parents and younger siblings moved to Thailand to begin missionary work there. That was entirely too exciting an opportunity to pass up, so I took a semester off from school to join them. A couple of months after arriving, I met a missionary who had been there several years. He had pictures everywhere—on the walls, in albums, and on slides. His talent for grasping images on film was captivating!

I had just purchased my first 35mm camera, so this

of the pie is made up of women. Also, being a Warrior does not mean you are an extrovert—the life of the party, energized by being around lots of people. Men and women can be wired as Warriors and yet be very quiet, private people.

So what *does* define a Warrior? At its core, the soul of a Warrior is motivated to conquer, to reach for a vision and obtain it by any good means possible. In today's language, Warriors are goal oriented. They are achievers. They don't want to talk about doing things; they just want to do them. For Warriors, the world is a battle to be won. Decisions are made with a sharp-edged clarity between right and wrong; there is no middle ground. Warriors are emotionally steady, courageous, and practical.

generous Artist took me under his wing and taught me the craft. I got up early one morning, and we spent all day floating the klongs—the canals that crisscrossed Bangkok. After snapping hundreds of shots and getting them developed, we pored over each one, noting the message of the image, the lighting, the composition. We discussed how each shot could be improved by cropping the image or using a different focal length.

That experience and that relationship brought something to life in me. Something that allowed me to connect and communicate in new ways. My life had received greater beauty from an Artist.

The Artist

What burns inside the creative soul of the Artist? Fundamentally, the Artist is motivated to communicate, to connect with the hearts of other men and women. The Artist wants to convey to others the passions he or she experiences. The world of the Artist is a canvas waiting to be painted with infinite shades of color. Not content simply to do, Artists are deeply inclined to understand—to wrestle with the meaning of ideas, events, and relationships. Artists are creative and expressive, more at home with ideas and concepts than the pragmatic matters of life. While they tend toward a more turbulent and moody inner life, Artists release their passion in a way that brings beauty to all who journey alongside them.

GUARDING THE DOWNSIDE

Artists and Warriors both exhibit wonderful qualities that bear enormously on how spouses form a unique partnership in marriage. And both personality types possess propensities toward a number of weaknesses.

Warriors find it easy to be critical of others who don't see things the way they do or who are passive in the face of injustice. In contrast, Artists find it easier to be critical of themselves and may be reluctant to make decisions, or they second-guess the decisions they've already made.

The Warrior can be overly confrontational in conflict and must resist the urge to control people and circumstances. In contrast, the Artist tends to withdraw and avoid confrontation, even when the issue at hand may be worth contending for.

While the Warrior may neglect or injure people as she pursues the conquest that ignites her passion, the Artist may become so focused on people and process that he doesn't accomplish necessary tasks.

Finally, the Warrior's strength can lead her to be overly independent from others, while the Artist's creativity can lead him to be overly dependent on others. The goal of both soul types should be a healthy *interdependence* of give-and-take that fosters mutual respect and teamwork.

The following chart highlights the essential contrasts between the two.

It should be apparent by now that Artists and Warriors *need one another.* The strengths of one naturally cover the weaknesses of the other. Within every marriage, even marriages in which both husband and wife would identify with the same profile, one partner is going to be more Warrior and the other more Artist. This allows for the beauty of interplay and mutuality in the relationship.

WARRIOR		ARTIST
	How you're wired	
to conquer, to achieve	*Central Motivation*	to communicate, to connect
justice	*Core Value*	meaning
the world is a battle!	*Worldview*	the world is a canvas!
practical	*Soul Processing*	conceptual
steady, decisive	*Soul Structure*	variable, moody
	How you relate	
courageous, discerning	*Strengths*	creative, expressive
critical of others	*Weaknesses*	critical of self
confrontational, controlling	*Conflict*	nonconfrontational, withdrawing
independent, competitive	*Relational Tendency*	dependent, contemplative
focused outward	*Community Orientation*	focused inward

[Jerome] Recognizing that you are a Warrior and I'm an Artist has, I think, helped us understand each other. It helps us know what to expect of each other, and it helps us avoid trying to change each other's essential wiring. Our characteristics are there by design. Of course, we each keep maturing and forming our souls toward the image of Christ. We reach for the grace to grow in our areas of weakness so we can more clearly reflect the life of God.

But because you are a Warrior and I am an Artist, your strengths cover my weaknesses, and I'm able to cover your weaknesses at important times.

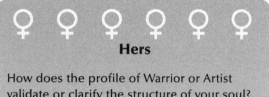

Hers

How does the profile of Warrior or Artist validate or clarify the structure of your soul? What new insights have you gained into your makeup as you consider yourself in light of being an Artist or Warrior?

The ability to understand the structure of each other's soul opens up the capacity to communicate and move as a team. It affects how we minister, how we parent, how we work, how we make love… Every facet of our lives is influenced by the design God used when he imagined us and created us as Warriors or Artists.

[Kellie] I remember how much it helped me when we took a personality profile test that broke people into four categories and labeled them as various animals. It validated me on a practical level and helped me understand and accept myself more fully. But the Warrior and Artist concept takes us into the spiritual realm, where we're describing not just the shape of our personalities but the contours of our souls.

[Jerome] Are you saying that who we are as Warriors and Artists carries us into the realm of spiritual calling and giftedness?

[Kellie] Yes, it includes giftedness and calling. And it's even an indicator of destiny. This is how God has wired us for the Kingdom. It's not just about how we appear to others or how we interact with others but how we bear Kingdom purpose on the earth, how we display God's glory.

It begins with personality but then picks up spiritual overtones. *Warrior* and *Artist* describe a good bit about our respective roles in the Kingdom. The Warrior is there to lead spiritual battles, to look ahead and discern what's on God's heart, to see where we're headed, to birth Kingdom values on

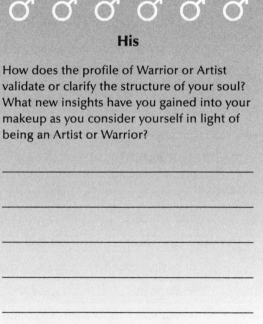

His

How does the profile of Warrior or Artist validate or clarify the structure of your soul? What new insights have you gained into your makeup as you consider yourself in light of being an Artist or Warrior?

_____

_____

_____

_____

_____

the earth. I really believe this is a Warrior's role in the spiritual
dimension of life.

[Jerome] And the Artist has a spiritual calling to perceive the beauty
of God's design and amplify the heart of God in creative ways
to all who will listen. God calls Artists to give expression and
persuasion to the passions of God—to communicate the
heartbeat of heaven.

Partnership, as we envision it, is about much more than learning how
the Artist and Warrior can get along in spite of their differences. When we
begin to really grasp each other's spiritual gifting, calling, and destiny, then
we find the potential to reach a potent agreement and accomplish heavenly
tasks together. To understand yourself and your partner is just the beginning; from there, you have to go somewhere and become something as a team
that is true to your Kingdom purpose.

In some sense, we'll be marked by our calling as Warriors and Artists
even in heaven. It's part of God's custom imprint upon the eternal soul of
men and women; it's part of uncovering who we are as God sees us.

WHEN RUBBER MEETS THE ROAD

[Kellie] So what's it like to live as an Artist for the Kingdom? I know
that you're an idea person.

[Jerome] Yeah. Sometimes I feel bombarded by ideas. I always seem
to have more ideas than I could ever practically pursue. So
perhaps the challenge facing a godly Artist is to figure out
which ideas come from God and which are stirred by an over-
active imagination. Artists need to identify the ideas that have
the breath of heaven on them.

And then there's a timing issue, and that's where you help me a lot. When I get a great new idea—even a God-inspired idea—I want to leap into it immediately. But you usually have a good sense of timing and strategy about when to initiate new things.

[Kellie] And you're very concerned about communicating vision.

[Jerome] Absolutely. It burns in me to see where God wants to take us, in the family or in the church or in the Kingdom, and then paint that picture for people, whether I'm using the canvas of a book or a song or a sermon. As a life coach, I'm continually helping people clarify their own direction and purpose. I want to fire people's imagination with a hunger for something that is heavenly. I want to inspire them, equip them, and lead them to lay hold of that vision. This is definitely what motivates my life.

[Kellie] As a Warrior, I have vision as well, but I'm not motivated so much to communicate that vision as to make it happen. I don't always know exactly what's supposed to happen or how…but I have an impatience to change the status quo and reach for something new. It may be prayer, a new kind of worship, a different form of music, or reaching out to the community. Whatever I feel God wants us to do, I just want to do it.

WHERE DO YOU FALL ON THE SPECTRUM BETWEEN WARRIOR AND ARTIST?		
100% W	50% W	0% W
0% A	50% A	100% A

But I have to deal with the timing issue as well. Sometimes Warriors see things that God wants to bring about in the future so that we can intercede for them. Then it becomes a spiritual warring to bring that future forward. God gives Warriors a farsightedness so they can see what God desires, but seeing it and acting on it are two different things. Sometimes God gives Warriors a vision, and he wants them first to pray for God's will to become reality, rather than jumping in immediately to make it happen.

[Jerome] We both help each other at different times with matters of timing—knowing what to do with what we feel. I often need to be motivated to put my ideas into action, and sometimes my role is to rein in your propensity to action.

[Kellie] We've been in meetings together where ten people were throwing around ideas, talking, rehashing…and you just love it. You're in your element working with concepts. But I feel like I'm either shriveling up or about to explode. I can't stand it. To me it feels like meaningless jabber. I want to say, "Stop talking about it! Let's all get out and do something about it!"

I know it's good to work things through and make plans before taking action, but my soul is chomping at the bit. It's like when I have a picture to hang. I grab a hammer and a nail, and I drive it into the wall. But you get out the measuring tape and the level. For you it's a process; for me it's an accomplishment.

[Jerome] Artists are more process oriented in general. I don't know if Artists actually process things any better than Warriors, but they have more appreciation for it. Warriors just want to get it done; *how* is negotiable.

I'd say an appreciation of process is important because of the value God places on people. When action and achieving a goal are the only things that matter, people can get chewed up, injured, and lost. Warriors and Artists together have to guard against people getting lost in the focus on either process or action. In so many ways, people *are* the goal!

[Kellie] Relationships are important to both Warriors and Artists, but they look at them differently. Artists are probably more drawn to see people as the goal, and Warriors are drawn to see people as the means to accomplish goals. I think both are true, and we need one another so we don't fall into extremes on either end.

That's the beauty of partnership: things are done well when you work together. You avoid the danger of the Artist processing things to death and the equal danger of the Warrior getting things done but doing them less wisely. But while partnership is empowering, it's not always easy. Because the Warrior and Artist look at the same situation through such different lenses, there is usually an implicit conflict between their perspectives. Each of us needs humility and a commitment to the partnership that allows one or both of us to sacrifice our natural inclinations for the benefit of the team.

QUESTIONS FOR PRAYER AND CONVERSATION

1. In what ways have you seen the church define gender-related roles and functions in ways that reflect cultural tradition more than Scripture?

2. Have you ever felt that you didn't fit the popular stereotypes that commonly define your gender?

3. Where do the descriptions of Warrior and Artist shine a light on you: weaknesses to be covered or strengths to be released?

Myself

Familiar stranger I am to me
Caught in the currents I know
Pressing against the boundaries I see
Yet formed by the ones that I don't

Hung between visions I see down the range
And the patterns I occupy now
My soul journeys on and I know that there's change
Though it's fuzzy just when and just how

I know who I am and yet I'm surprised
Sometimes the old stranger appears
Sometimes the parts that I've secretly prized
Are the parts that reduce me to tears

Who can make sense of this one called myself?
Surely the One by design
Who crafted my soul and calls me to Himself
And placed your hand in mine

Together we'll journey this road that's before us
Together make sense of ourselves
Blending your verse and mine in a rising chorus
A little less strange to myself

warriors and artists
in partnership

*Making Sense of the Four Possible
Combinations in Marriage*

OUR FAMILY was having lunch on the deck one afternoon, and I (Jerome) had dashed inside to answer the phone. Being the Artist I am, I'm much more of a phone person than Kellie is. Since I'm motivated to connect, I can imagine sitting face to face with a person who is actually hundreds of miles away. While I was inside "connecting" over the phone, our neighbor's dog got loose and came careening around the side of the house and onto our deck.

The dog was a new addition to the neighborhood. I couldn't tell you what kind it was except that it was big and black and loud. More to the point, my three young kids were terrified of it. As it clambered noisily onto the deck, barking and growling, the kids screamed and shrank back. The Warrior, however, did not. I looked outside just in time to see Thorpe's tricycle leaving Kellie's hands and hurtling through the air, aimed squarely at the dog. Kellie stopped shouting at the intruder long enough to push the kids through the back door and into the house, where they stood, shaken and crying.

The commotion had aroused the dog's owner, who came running into our yard. Kellie stayed inside the house, not trusting herself to speak civilly to the neighbor. Meanwhile, Mr. Artist disengaged from the phone conversation and went outside to connect with the neighbor. The man was apologetic and tried to convince us that the dog was harmless. But you couldn't tell that to my three scared kids...or to the Warrior watching over them. I have no doubt that had a gun been within reach, the dog's next occupation would have been pushing up daisies.

The Forces That Make Us

A great deal of who you are as a husband or a wife is shaped by your "Warriorness" or "Artistness." It's great to find yourself described in a personality profile and gain greater insight into how you're wired. But it's an even more powerful tool as it relates to your marriage. Your communication style, your leadership style, your values and motivations all reflect the fundamental orientation of your soul. What does it mean to be a Warrior or an Artist in marriage?

The Effect of the Past
Your marriage is shaped by a number of forces in addition to the role played by your personality. Your *history* is a big one. The experiences you

have had, the wounds of the past, the heroes in your life, your home environment growing up—you bring all these influences with you into marriage. The hard part is understanding how your past shaped you and how you continue to play out that identity. An essential component of marriage preparation is to meet over a period of time with a counselor who can help you understand yourself and your prospective spouse.

You wouldn't want to run a ten-kilometer race wearing ankle weights. And yet every marriage brings two people together who carry within them injuries and fears from the past. Your history includes damage to your self-image, which weighs you down with lies about God, lies about other people, and lies about yourself. These forces from the past form a grid of influences that filters the way you speak and act.

Because each of us still feels the sting of past injuries, we develop protective strategies to defend ourselves from being hurt again. These subconscious shields warp our understanding of our God-given design and undermine our potential for full partnership and freedom of soul with the one we love. Wise spouses cultivate a lifelong vigilance against the ongoing threat of past hurts and gratefully receive God's help. So take advantage of empowering resources such as counseling, the Scriptures, Christian books, mentors, and friends.

The Impact of Gender

Another major force that shapes your interaction with life and love is your innate masculinity or femininity. While we have made constant reference to the equality of men and women, as well as the absence of biblically defined gender roles, that is not to say that men and women are the same! Men and women possess unique marks of God, which means we communicate his image in different ways. Gender doesn't define what we do, but it does to a large extent define who we are. Gender helps shape personality, and personality shapes the expression of gender. There is a marvelous, mysterious interplay between the two.

The differences in gender begin, of course, with physiology. Namely, the woman is uniquely shaped by her ability to bear children, and the man is uniquely shaped by his physical strength. These attributes are alluded to as God declares the consequences of the Fall: "Your womanhood, Eve, will bear the sinful consequence of pain in childbirth. Your manhood, Adam, will bear the sinful consequence of pain in your physical labor." It's true that women also share the challenge of a cursed earth and its resistance to productive labor; however, God directs this comment toward Adam and highlights men's ability for physical labor.

But the consequences of sin go further than painful childbearing or constant hassles at work. After the Fall, Adam and Eve struggled relationally. The shape of their masculine and feminine souls predisposed Adam to domination and Eve to oppression. This reflects a psychological extension of their physiological distinctions, particularly when you look at the positive side.

Women are uniquely capable of bearing and nursing children, which imprints a woman's soul with a tendency toward nurture and protectiveness. A man's physical strength, which enables him to farm or fight, imprints his soul with initiative and conquest. Now, it's clear that all women are not equally nurturing and all men are not equally aggressive. It's also evident that men have a calling to partner with women in nurture and women have a calling to partner with men in conquest. Still, the bell-shaped curve for gender emphasizes these gender-specific qualities.

The Influence of Spiritual Gifts
Gender, personality, and personal history work together in a complex blend to make you who you are. These forces help shape your identity and

subsequently your close relationships. The final major shaping element is *spiritual gifting*. To each man and woman, irrespective of gender, God distributes a personalized mix of gifts that channel the work of the Holy Spirit through that person (see Romans 12 and 1 Corinthians 12). The spiritual gifts become tools for establishing God's Kingdom on the earth.

This simple diagram shows how four forces blend to shape a person's identity in a way that's not simple!

When you consider the way these forces intersect and interact to form your identity, it helps to clearly identify the four dynamics that continue to work within you. It also invites you to delve deeper into each of these dimensions and receive understanding from God about who you are and

FOUR FORCES THAT SHAPE YOUR INTERACTION IN MARRIAGE

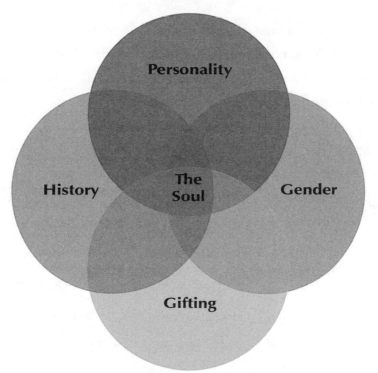

who you are meant to be. Furthermore, God wants to free your heart from restrictions, both internal and external, that try to force you into a mold that is not of his design. The more he reveals *his* idea and intent for who he created you to be, the more you can embrace his perfect idea and leave behind the masks and pretensions you're tempted to wear to gain acceptance and approval.

THE WARRIOR-ARTIST DYNAMIC IN MARRIAGE

You are a man or a woman with a particular history and a set of spiritual gifts. You are also a Warrior or an Artist who is married to a Warrior or an Artist. By now you're familiar with your own personality type, but how does the combination of your personality and your spouse's personality affect your marriage?

You and your spouse fall into one of four combinations: a Warrior married to a Warrior, an Artist married to an Artist, a Warrior husband married to an Artist wife, or a Warrior wife married to an Artist husband. Charted out, the four combinations look like this:

		Warrior	Wife	Artist
Warrior		**Quadrant I** Husband: Warrior Wife: Warrior		**Quadrant II** Husband: Warrior Wife: Artist
Husband		**Quadrant III** Husband: Artist Wife: Warrior		**Quadrant IV** Husband: Artist Wife: Artist
Artist				

What's certain is that the couples in each quadrant experience life, relationship, and partnership differently. On top of that, every couple is as unique as every individual is unique. Still, there are tendencies in each quadrant toward certain strengths and weaknesses, and it's important that you understand the tendencies. We conducted some informal research that, together with common sense, highlights some of the tendencies that are characteristic of each combination of married couples. Think through the quadrant that represents your marriage (or future marriage), and see how it may cast a new light on your experience.

Quadrant I: You're Both Warriors

The Warrior married to a Warrior is a combination that is both powerful and volatile! The strength of your personalities opens up the possibility for greater friction but also an amazing strength of purpose. When you bring your vision into alignment with your spouse's vision, nothing can stand in your way. Your strengths show up in the ability to get things done, whether it's money management, parenting, setting priorities—you name it. Your weaknesses show up in *how* you get there.

Leadership and communication are often challenging for two Warriors. You will probably have to work harder than other couples to learn how your respective strengths complement one another. When you hit a sticking point and get into a disagreement, the temperature can rise quickly. Your spiritual lives can sometimes be a challenge as well because you both have a goal-oriented nature. Yet the Kingdom calling for two Warriors is to revel in one another's strength, build an effective process for merging your passions, cultivate close friendships with a few Artists who can help you stay grounded, and then release the multiplied power of your unity in the different facets of your partnership.

Quadrant II: He's a Warrior, She's an Artist

This combination tends to find the easiest fit in marriage. If you are a Warrior husband married to an Artist wife, your personality types conform most closely to the gender expectations of Western society. As a result, your interactions with each other and your joint decision making may come more easily. The unspoken affirmation of culture provides a strong subconscious boost to this configuration.

That doesn't mean your relationship won't take work, however. The challenge you face is to not allow cultural currents to reinforce separate domains in your marriage. Don't allow yourselves to be relegated to worlds that are more apart than together. Your reach for true partnership in marriage might be far more of a stretch than it is for other couples.

The tendency toward separate domains sometimes has an adverse effect on the spiritual relationship of couples in your configuration, because spiritual connection requires a high degree of integration in each other's worlds. You may have to rely on more intentional structures to create regular times for prayer and spiritual interaction. The ability to connect emotionally on a deep level, to reinforce equality in your teamwork, and to communicate effectively in your partnership are the skills you need to intentionally pursue. Yet the Kingdom calling for a Warrior man and an Artist woman is to take advantage of your natural complementariness to move purposefully toward partnership at home, in ministry, and in the workplace.

Quadrant III: He's an Artist, She's a Warrior

This configuration is the flip of the previous combination, and the strengths and weaknesses are flipped as well. Finding your fit in marriage will perhaps be the most challenging of the four combinations. But when you do find it, you, perhaps more than any other configuration, have the opportunity for a powerful partnership. The Warrior side of the woman balances her femininity with some characteristics that may be considered masculine—a willingness to confront, the drive toward achieving goals, the tendency to take initiative. Similarly, we might say that the Artist man is "in touch with his feminine side," yet this does not imply that he is either weak or soft—only that his strength shows itself in more relational ways.

This dynamic creates an inner struggle for both of you as you reach to understand yourselves and embrace your God-given design. However, because these personality forces shift both of you toward the center of the gender spectrum, it releases a potent opportunity for enhanced partnership.

Your spiritual connection will likely come easier than for other couples because of this "centered" dynamic. The husband's relational bent and the wife's motivation for nurture coalesce in a mutual desire for connection. Meanwhile, channels of effective leadership will require more effort initially due to the subconscious cultural pressure that works against the Warrior wife–Artist husband combination. It may take this couple more time to develop good structures and practices in the areas of leadership and communication.

The work arena, in particular, presents unique challenges that may result in conflict. The wife may be more motivated or effective in the marketplace than her husband. Some couples find this to be a challenge; others don't. But don't be deterred. God has powerful plans for you if your marriage falls into this quadrant. The Kingdom calling for the Artist man and the Warrior woman is to embrace your uniqueness of soul individually and then tap the full potential of Kingdom authority that flows naturally out of your partnership. Because this particular configuration experiences distinct dynamics, we will spend more time discussing Warrior women and Artist men in the next chapter.

Quadrant IV: You're Both Artists

When an Artist man marries an Artist woman, it produces a colorful, unpredictable relationship marked by exuberant passion and creative spontaneity! The drive to communicate and connect tends to result in, well, good communication and connection. Both relationally and spiritually, there will be a natural desire to do whatever it takes to get on the same page. On the emotional side, it may feel like a roller coaster, given the artistic temperament of you both. And when it comes to conflict, look out! The strengths of two Artists can create as much tension as the Warrior-Warrior combination. Yet when partnership emerges, the sky is the limit on the potential for communicating a creative message to the world.

Potential weaknesses include how you handle money, how you live out your priorities, and the need to take initiative. Just as the Warrior-Warrior couple needs close friendship with Artists to bring balance, so the Artist-Artist couple needs close friends who are Warriors to help bring focus and motivation.

The parenting style of the Artist dad and Artist mom will predispose you to good relational connection with your children but could also open the door to undue permissiveness. In sum, the Kingdom calling for the Artist man married to an Artist woman is to revel in the beauty of life together, help anchor each other in the moody moments, and release the explosive potential of your creativity and skill in communicating God's heart.

RESHAPING THE PROCESS

Having a vision for oneness, authority, and partnership in marriage is one thing. Getting there is another.

Many couples passionately yearn for partnership yet still get bogged down in the process. Vision is all about the destination: *where* you are going together. Mission is all about the journey: *how* you will get where you're going. The secret to a successful mission is anticipating obstacles and creating processes for negotiating those obstacles while maintaining a keen unity of heart.

Every healthy relationship encounters conflict. For Warrior-Warrior and Artist-Artist marriages, the conflicts may be spectacular, but it's all part of the fabric of life. Because spouses retain their individuality and personality in the oneness of marriage, it's no surprise that conflicting perspectives, feelings, and motivations arise. Differing views and feelings are genuine, authentic to who each spouse is. To ignore or deny the differences is to lose something of yourself, which you instinctively don't want to do. Thus, the conflict.

Conflict in itself is not a bad thing. The question is where does conflict take you? Does it take you toward more complete partnership or away from partnership? All destructive conflict flows out of one or more of the three root sins: fear, greed, and pride.

Perhaps you fear that you will be invalidated as a person, that your feelings will be disregarded, and that you'll lose respect or worth. So you fight with even greater force to defend against what you see as a threat to your personhood.

Or maybe, at times, greed motivates you to grasp after power in the relationship. You sense that your spouse is gaining the upper hand in some aspect of your marriage, and your competitive nature kicks in. You want equality in a legalistic sense, like a pie that is cut *precisely* down the middle before portions are given out. So your conflict takes on an added layer of passion—and perhaps volume.

And always there is the potential for pride to motivate you to think of your views, ideas, goals, and perceptions as superior to those of your spouse.

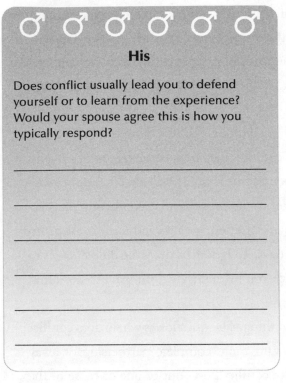

His

Does conflict usually lead you to defend yourself or to learn from the experience? Would your spouse agree this is how you typically respond?

_____

_____

_____

_____

_____

_____

You have more confidence—or familiarity—in yourself than you do in your spouse, so you elevate your opinion above that of your partner.

In a very real sense, the solution to all destructive conflict is the Cross of Jesus—the empowering grace of God to conquer our sin and release his righteous responses within us.

But conflict doesn't have to be a bad thing. Conflict can unwrap new potential in your marriage. We believe the key to redemptive conflict lies in something very simple: seeing conflict as an opportunity to learn. Drs. Jordan and Margaret Paul identify two, and only two, responses to conflict. A spouse responds either out of a motivation to protect himself or out of a desire to learn;[15] this perspective alone has made a big difference in our relationship. And the choice you make at this crucial juncture will make all the difference in the world in _your_ marriage!

Choosing Life

What are couples supposed to learn through conflict? It's a great question, with several possible answers. First, you have the opportunity to learn something about yourself. None of us fully knows our own hearts, and many times we respond to situations instinctively…but don't really grasp what triggers our response. So conflict becomes a chance to ask yourself, *What am I really feeling? Why do I feel this so strongly? This feeling is authentic, but is it godly? Is it true to God's perspective?* Asking questions such as these invites God's Spirit to come inside with his gentle illumination to show you your heart.

Second, you have the opportunity to learn something about your spouse. Without rushing to assume you know his or her motivation—and then judge it—you can ask your spouse: "What makes you feel this way? What is it about my perspective that rubs you wrong? Why does this situation trigger such strong emotion in your heart?"

Of course, attitude is everything. If you ask these questions in a defensive or accusatory tone, you have chosen the path of self-protection rather than the path of humility. Timing is another key issue. If emotions have flared, you may need to let them simmer down before coming back to try to learn from the situation.

A third opportunity to learn from conflict arises when you discover that your respective goals are actually identical but you see different paths to get there. In this case, conflict highlights your strengths rather than weaknesses. Or another way of saying it is, the weakness you are reacting against may be the flip side of your spouse's strength. When you

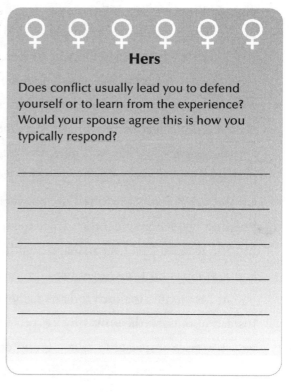

Hers

Does conflict usually lead you to defend yourself or to learn from the experience? Would your spouse agree this is how you typically respond?

recognize that dynamic, it's a prime opportunity to release your partner's strength by validating it. At this point, you have the opportunity to bring your joint strengths and perspectives to bear upon your mutual goal. This is one way that conflict becomes an avenue to increased partnership.

Here's a personal example. A little while back I (Jerome) decided to wait tables at an upscale restaurant to help fill some financial gaps while our ministry was getting off the ground. After several days of training, it was my first day to take tables without assistance. When I arrived at work, the other waiters were engaged in a good-natured debate over who would take a party of twelve older gentlemen who were known to be finicky and demanding.

"I had them last time!" one girl said.

"Well, it's my birthday," said one of the guys, "and that's not the kind of present I'm looking for!"

Looking for a chance to prove myself, I jumped in. "Well, I'm new. I'll give it a shot." It was a shot I came to regret!

I actually did a fair job of taking down each guy's order, getting them into the computer system, and even delivering the right food to the right people. The problem came when it was time to split the check twelve ways. I asked a veteran waitress, "How do you split the checks again?" She pointed me to the right computer screen, but in the process I managed to get the seat assignments mixed up. So when the separate checks were run, I wound up charging half the men's credit cards for somebody else's meal! It was a disaster. I had the manager in a frenzy trying to correct my mess, and I wondered if I might get fired on the spot.

As I recounted the story later to Kellie, she began to get upset with me. Instead of offering the sympathy I expected, she was angry. "Tell me again why you felt compelled to take a group of twelve on your first day?" she asked. I was hurt and became defensive, attempting to protect myself from what felt like an undeserved assault. In other words, we did it wrong before we did it right!

But then we chose to learn from our conflict. We stretched past our own skin saving and sought instead to gain information and understanding. In the midst of our argument, some glimmers of truth began to surface. Kellie felt that I had given in to old patterns of people pleasing by accepting the table that other servers wanted to avoid. But eventually I was able to articulate my motivation: I wanted to challenge some of my innate risk aversion by not playing it safe. Instead, I took a gamble and went for it! Even though I lost the gamble rather spectacularly, I wasn't sure that it hadn't been a noble venture. When Kellie saw it from that perspective, her attitude changed 180 degrees. Learning triumphed over self-protection.

Learning from times of conflict requires each partner to rein in his or her destructive tendencies. For Warriors, it means clamping down on the instinct to conquer and prevail. For Artists, it means resisting the inclination to withdraw and hide or, alternatively, to acquiesce simply to keep the peace. These three pathologies—conquering, withdrawing, and acquiescing[16]—are equally destructive to your relationship. It's crucial that you identify them and deal with them. Humility and courage are the spiritual qualities that empower you to avoid the pitfalls and choose a life-giving attitude of learning in the midst of conflict.

Conflict is inherently polarizing, making you feel your spouse is the enemy. "If he would just wise up and see what I'm saying, we could get past this!" At this point, conflict degenerates into an argument where each of you is seeking to win. But regardless of who wins the argument, both of you lose.

If our different perspectives on the restaurant scene had not come to light, and if we hadn't been able to appreciate both sides of the issue, we would have chalked up yet another incident of aggravation, animosity, and hurt...without anything positive to show for it. Instead, God helped us choose the path of learning and gain deeper understanding and greater appreciation for each other.

At any point in the process, one partner can make an appeal for perspective and reframe the conflict redemptively. In this way you are moving from opposing sides of the fence to the *same* side of the fence. When I was telling Kellie about my restaurant debacle, there was a critical shift where we stopped criticizing each other and began to reach for a common understanding. When this happened, the focus and the tone of the conversation shifted totally. If you can make the shift, partnership is restored and your relationship renewed! This is the power of partnership for both Warriors and Artists.

QUESTIONS FOR PRAYER AND CONVERSATION

1. How well do you understand the ways in which your identity has been formed by your history, your gender, your personality, and your spiritual gifts? How well do you understand how those same influences affect your marriage?

2. What combination of personality types describes your relationship? How does this configuration affect your partnership?

3. What is your default mode in times of conflict? What is your spouse's default mode? Have you been able to redirect conflict so that it becomes an opportunity for learning and greater understanding?

AFFIRMING THE
"ODD COUPLE"

The Beauty of Women Warriors and Men Artists

AS AN ARTIST, I (Jerome) have always been drawn to literature and music. As a young teenager, I was leading worship in small groups and playing electric bass in the church band on Wednesday nights. It wasn't so much the music itself that captured my imagination; it was the power of music to create a spiritual connection—both horizontally and vertically—that compelled me. The nearness to God and the camaraderie of people gripped me as a young man…and led me to be a worship pastor for ten years.

The draw toward books also began at a young age. Throughout grade school, if I wasn't out combing the woods or riding my bicycle, I was tucked into a ball in my "reading chair"—the wing chair with the gold and avocado floral design in the living room. It wasn't all classical literature, to be sure, but the power that words and stories possessed to draw me into magical experiences imprinted my soul.

I was marked as an Artist, but it took the stillness of a Colorado sabbatical to allow the quiet murmurings of my heart to surface and be heard, to be tended and then released in writing. The radical surgery of soul that took place in the early months of a Rocky Mountain summer began to cry for expression. And so I expressed it. Without knowing how my writing would ever be published, I began to write...telling our story. I was reaching, looking for connection, driven to communicate our discoveries.

The quest for beauty. And the yearning to share that beauty with another soul. This is the heart of an Artist.

MINORITY SYNDROME

In chapter 8 we talked about the four combinations of personalities in marriage, and in this chapter we want to talk in detail about one configuration in particular—a Warrior woman married to an Artist man. These couples face unique issues and obstacles while at the same time they enjoy unique opportunities.

We can speak to the Artist man–Warrior woman configuration authentically because it's who we are. We have experienced firsthand the challenges and the opportunities of finding our fit with one another. The first challenge that couples like us face is the feeling that in our marriage the traditional roles have flip-flopped. The Warrior woman has a strong soul and is characterized by a strong sense of justice and a willingness to contend for that justice. More than other women, she will assert herself and take initiative in opposing what is wrong. The Artist man, on the other hand, applies his strength in more expressive and relational ways, compared to other men.

Because both of these personalities are in the minority within their respective gender, their marriage falls into minority status as well…or at least the *perception* of minority status. As this personality-gender combination in marriage finds broader affirmation, we will see that this configuration represents a significant segment of the married population.

In churches where marital roles are more tightly defined, the expectations bleed over from role to personality. Men are expected not only to lead the family but also to have a take-charge, can-do approach to life and ministry. Women are expected not only to take a submissive and responsive role in marriage but also to adopt a demure, self-effacing posture in general. Of course, this doesn't describe all churches.

But where this happens, Artist men and Warrior women are told—either indirectly or openly—that they shouldn't be the way they are. The message is this: "Your personality is all wrong, and you need to change!" The effect ranges from a subtle undermining of their worth to, even worse, a negation of their identity that sends them into years of trying to be someone they are not. A person can't change his innate wiring in order to conform to external expectations without suffering significant inner damage.

Trying to be who you're not sets up a conflict in your soul, because God made you a certain way. This inner conflict is there for a reason—to help you realize that God's design is good. God has made some women to be stronger in the expression of their souls than other women…or other men, for that matter. And God has designed some men to be more creative, more gifted in communicating than others.

It took me (Kellie) a long time to accept myself as a God-created Warrior woman. I struggled for years before I was able to appreciate the beauty of the way God wired my soul. I have undergone a gradual awakening to my role in the Kingdom, which is to make things happen, to champion God's passion for wise action in the earth. However you're wired, God wants to bring peace to your soul and to affirm his goodness in making you the way you are.

While some of these issues play out in the church, the real crucible for marriage is the home. When men and women in this configuration have not come to grips with the goodness of their personalities, it will cause dissonance in their souls and dissonance in their relationship. Finding their true fit will be elusive, to say the least.

Without authentic partnership, a Warrior wife will boss her husband and her kids. She will overwhelm her husband's need for processing with demands and preemptive decisions. And she will ultimately emasculate his worth and identity as a man. The Artist husband will, in turn, get lost in his creativity and in connecting with others and so neglect both the practical and relational needs of his family. He will place the weight of running the home entirely on his wife. Once this pattern is established, the habits of both spouses tend to reinforce a downward spiral of separation and alienation.

But the spiraling stops and partnership begins with understanding and appreciating each other's essential wiring. From there, you start to learn how to use tools that generate togetherness. The Warrior woman needs to actively seek her husband's wisdom for decisions and to honor his need to process things. The Artist man needs to harness his creative and social strengths and direct them toward the issues and needs that his wife discerns within the family. It's not complicated, but it requires tenacity to carve out new habits of communication and teamwork.

The key is setting aside regular times for talking and praying through these issues together. Most answers won't come from a book; they come directly from God. So it requires an active engagement with God and each other to listen and work through the practical matters of partnership. This is true for all personality combinations in marriage and certainly for this one.

MISFIT NO MORE

[Kellie] If God really has created some men as Artists and some
women as Warriors and placed us in marriage together, then
God has a particular place for us in the Kingdom. A unique,
special place. Although we may feel at times as though we're
misfits, we need to know that God has prepared a powerful
purpose for our marriage. And it's up to us to find out what
that purpose is.

[Jerome] We talked before about how men and women tend toward
a few gender-specific attributes. God created humanity as man
and woman because in masculinity and femininity we express
his heart and his nature in the world. So another way to describe this truth is to say that you can be a Warrior woman
and still be fully feminine. And I can be an Artist man and be
fully masculine. There is no conflict. But as is the case with
any personality, we need to identify and understand our
innate weaknesses and grow in light of them. We need to receive the grace of God to move toward maturity. In this way
we will use our personality not as a license for selfish, destructive behavior but as a channel for the life of God.

Women as Warriors

[Kellie] When people think of a Warrior, they probably get a mental
image of Mel Gibson in *Braveheart* or Russell Crowe in *Gladi-
ator.* They might picture weapons and violence, blood and

sweat—very masculine images. But what I love about Warrior
women is that they can burn for justice and strive for godly
change and still move in a very feminine way.

[Jerome] For one thing, Christian warfare takes place primarily in the
spiritual realm. So Warriors aren't usually called to confront
people; they're called to confront spiritual enemies.

[Kellie] Yes, the spiritual realm is the primary battlefield. But there
are times when we do have to confront people. And when
that's necessary, it comes more naturally for Warriors than
Artists. For example, we were in the grocery store the other
day. We were walking out, and you looked at the receipt and
thought we had been overcharged. I felt we needed to go back
and tell them.

[Jerome] So I handed you the receipt, and you went back and
worked it out. You weren't in their face, you didn't get overly
aggressive, but you didn't mind appealing for justice.

[Kellie] On the other hand, I remember being in the doctor's office
and getting all worked up over how long we were having to
wait. I was really angry; I guess it felt like an injustice at the
time. You helped me see that it wouldn't be good to confront
them. I wouldn't have done it in a godly way! But you were
able to talk to them without getting upset, and that was a
moment of partnership.

Another characteristic of Warriors is that we tend to be very
protective. Of course, mothers are naturally protective of their
children, but if you're a Warrior, the protective drive is multiplied.
If you hurt my children, I'll get in your face. I don't have to think
about it; it's just instinctive.

I went to the mall one day with a friend. Our kids were having fun in a play area, which had a low wall around it. My friend and I were sitting at a table nearby, and kids were everywhere, running and climbing and screaming. We were talking and keeping an eye on the boys as they played. Just as I glanced over at Thorpe, who was three or four at the time, I saw an older boy hitting him and slapping him in the face.

I sprinted from the table, jumped the wall, and grabbed that kid. I got in his face and said, "I don't know what your problem is, but you'd better stop hitting my son!" That's the response of a Warrior! I know most mothers are protective of their children, but if you're a Warrior, that dynamic is turbocharged.

When I'm hanging out with my sisters or my friends, I find that they look to me to say something or do something. If we're at a restaurant and the food is taking too long or the server messes up the order, everyone expects me to work it out.

[Jerome] One of the things I appreciate about you is that even though you have a strong soul, you always carry yourself in a decisively feminine way. I have seen some Warrior women move in a way that felt, to me, unfeminine. They were hyperaggressive, as if they were trying to be masculine in their strength. I believe God invites women to be strong and at the same time gracious and spiritual and feminine. When this happens, they reveal the glory of God through their womanhood.

Several women in the Bible stand out as Warriors. You can feel the strength of their souls and their passion for justice. One great example is Miriam, the sister of Moses and Aaron. The Bible says, "Indeed, I brought you [the Israelites] up from the land of Egypt…, and I sent before you Moses, Aaron and Miriam" (Micah 6:4, NASB).

Miriam was a key leader of the Hebrews, helping to lead the slaves out of Egypt and into their promised land. She's one of the first worship leaders we see in Scripture, leading thousands in the praise of God. Her Warrior strength actually exceeded her character at one point and got her into trouble when she challenged Moses (see Numbers 12). But God's rebuke brought restoration, and her strength remained a great influence for good among God's people.

Then you have women such as Deborah, the prophetess and judge, who, together with Barak, led God's people in war to throw off the tyranny of oppressive nations (see Judges 4 and 5). There is Esther, who appears to have been more of an introvert, probably a very quiet woman. But on the

The Shunammite Woman

One of my (Kellie's) favorite Old Testament stories involves the Shunammite woman and the prophet Elisha (see 2 Kings 4). This woman recognized God's anointing on Elisha, so much so that she and her husband built a guest room on the roof of their house, where Elisha stayed when he traveled through their area. After being served by the hospitality of the Shunammite and her husband, Elisha asked her what he could do to reward her kindness. The woman was barren, and Elisha prophesied that within the year she would hold a son in her arms.

God made good on his word, and she gave birth to a son. The boy grew up and became the joy of his mother's inside, she had the heart of a lion. She seized the opportunity to contend for her people and oppose the injustice that threatened their survival (see the book of Esther).

Another woman I (Kellie) like comes from the New Testament. There's a quick story in Matthew 15 about a Canaanite woman. She was a Gentile, but she still approached Jesus to ask him to heal her daughter. This Warrior mother clearly had tremendous faith in Jesus's power, even though it was likely she didn't totally understand who he was. She knew enough to realize that he was the answer to her need.

But Jesus was unusually hard on this woman. First he ignored her pleas. Then he rebuked her, saying his ministry was for the Jews. But she

heart. But then he suddenly grew sick and died! The Shunammite was devastated.

The distraught woman told her husband that she must travel to the prophet. She seemed to be gripped by the sense of injustice in her son's death, and she needed God to make it right. When she reached Elisha, she cried out, "Did I ask you for a son, my lord? Didn't I tell you, 'Don't raise my hopes'?" (2 Kings 4:28). The passion and determination of her Warrior soul got results. The prophet Elisha returned to her home and raised her son back to life.

If the Shunammite had not been a Warrior, if she had not felt that injustice so deeply and then acted on it, she would never have received back her son. But God had created her to be a woman of action!

wouldn't quit; she knelt before him and said, "Lord, help me!" Jesus responded, "It is not right to take the children's bread and toss it to their dogs" (Matthew 15:26). It was a further putoff, but still she refused to back down.

She actually agreed with Jesus. "Yes, Lord," she replied, "but even the dogs eat the crumbs that fall from their masters' table." To which Jesus answered, "Woman, you have great faith! Your request is granted" (Matthew 15:27–28). Seeing this woman's Warrior heart go to war for her suffering daughter, Jesus finally commended her and honored her request. It's not easy to be a Warrior; there is a cost. But the way the Canaanite woman combined humility with strength is truly beautiful.

The woman in the New Testament who really strikes me (Jerome) as a Warrior is Martha, the sister of Mary and Lazarus. Martha tends to be viewed negatively because of the story where Mary was sitting at Jesus's feet and Martha was trying to force her back into the kitchen. This was not Martha's shining moment. But she did have a shining moment later. Martha and her brother and sister were three of Jesus's closest friends, and when Lazarus died, Jesus returned to their home for one of his most riveting miracles.

That's when Martha's Warrior spirit rose up: "Lord, if you had been here, my brother would not have died" (John 11:21). She was confronting God in the flesh! But her confidence in him shined at the same moment: "But I know that even now God will give you whatever you ask." This was an expression of amazing faith. In response, Jesus imparted a foundational pillar of truth: "I am the resurrection and the life. He who believes in me will live, even though he dies; and whoever lives and believes in me will never die. Do you believe this?" (John 11:25–26).

At this point Martha had a revelation, *the* revelation of all time: "I believe that you are the Christ, the Son of God, who was to come into the world" (John 11:27). Martha reached this point of revelation in large part because she was a Warrior…because she was willing to reach, to contend, to confront. Because she was bold and courageous.

Warrior women tend to see far ahead and grasp something of what God intends to do and then help birth that. They also have a strong gifting in the area of leadership. Whether introvert or extrovert, they want to take people somewhere. They're great delegators, very practical, and usually capable leaders. None of this is meant to minimize women who are Artists, women who display the beauty of Christ in a completely different dimension. But it's important to remember that Warrior women have lacked validation in the church and in society in general. Women who have been crafted this way by God should not try to hide or deny or change the way God has made them.

I (Kellie) have a close friend who is an Artist. She's a very mercy-motivated person. We get to minister together and pray for people together. I always love the way we flow with one another. I receive so much from her. The mercy and grace that ooze out of her combine with my Warrior nature in a beautiful way. The Kingdom of God needs Artists and Warriors working together in partnership.

Men as Artists

While gender predisposes men toward strength, it doesn't limit men to exercising their strength in warlike ways. Not all men are driven to conquer; some men are driven to connect.

It's tough these days for Artist men. So much of what is being written for Christian men calls them to be warriors. An Artist man could easily get the impression that since he's not a Type A, aggressive, spiritual commando, his masculinity is being questioned! To be sure, God calls every man to protect his family and to take responsibility—together with his wife—for the welfare of his home. And God doesn't want men to be wimps, to be passive and emotionally absent. But for Artist men, warring is what they do, not who they are.

Men are meant to be strong no matter what. They can be strong as Warriors, and they can be strong as Artists; the difference is the way their strength manifests itself. Where the strength of a Warrior man will be released to confront and conquer, the strength of an Artist man will be released to connect, to create, and to communicate. And these tasks require strength! A weak man can't connect and communicate effectively; this takes boldness, wisdom, and courage.

King Solomon was an Artist. God wouldn't let Solomon's father, King David, build his temple because David was a man of war. But God set Solomon apart to be a man of peace, and Solomon brought Israel into its golden years. This is one of the things that is so great about Artists: they thrive on beauty. Jerusalem under Solomon's rule was absolutely magnificent; he built the most beautiful, impressive buildings and gardens that Israel had ever seen.

When God asked Solomon early in his reign what one thing he most wanted, Solomon asked for wisdom (see 1 Kings 3:5–14), and wisdom marked his rule. As a

---

♀ ♀ ♀ ♀ ♀ ♀

Hers

Think of a Warrior woman–Artist man couple you know. How can you encourage and affirm their destiny in God?

_____

_____

_____

_____

_____

_____

---

wise judge, Solomon was very much the peacemaker. Part of being an Artist is being relational, and together with his passion for beauty, this translated into Solomon's surrounding himself with lots of wives, which, of course, became his downfall. But we can still appreciate the strength that was in him and how God used him to bring glory to his people.

Artist men will be captivated by beauty. It may be the beauty of a sunset that they paint or photograph, or it may be the beauty of the church—a vision they are driven to write about, speak about, or lead others toward. Or they might see the potential beauty of what marriage can be and then reach for that. Artists feel their strength and passion burning to declare a message, to take their inspiration and impart it to others. As we see in the life of Solomon, the strength of Artist men is directed to create and to build rather than to go to war.

Even though I (Kellie) am a Warrior, I've always been drawn to an Artist apostle in the New Testament. John is the only one of the Twelve described as "the disciple whom Jesus loved" (see John 13:23; 20:2; 21:7; 21:20). At the Last Supper, he's the one with his head on Jesus's chest. You can feel the special intimacy there. Even though Jesus was close to Peter and James, there was something different with John. You don't read about John

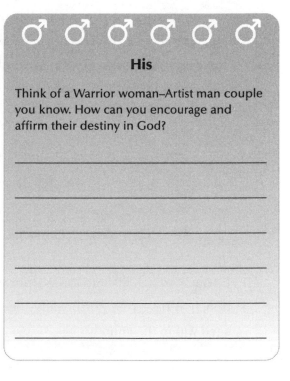

His

Think of a Warrior woman–Artist man couple you know. How can you encourage and affirm their destiny in God?

_____

_____

_____

_____

_____

_____

cutting off anyone's ear or being told, "Get behind me, Satan!" That just wasn't his personality.

John was an Artist and also a leader, an apostle well known to the churches of Asia Minor. He moved in tremendous authority throughout the early church, along with other leaders who were wired as Warriors— Peter, Paul, and others. John was the one God entrusted with the revelation of heaven and the last days.

But even before he wrote the book of Revelation, he had an amazing revelation himself of forgiveness, unity, transparency, and community. These come out strongly in his letters and reflect his motivation to see people connected to one another and to God.

The church needs both Artists and Warriors. The Kingdom of God needs both. God creates both personality types, and often he brings them together in marriage. So if you are a Warrior woman married to an Artist man, or vice versa, be encouraged. God has given you a special destiny. As you come into partnership in your marriage, and as God fits the two of you together as one, the authority and purpose of God will be released in your marriage and your ministry in amazing ways. Be who God made you to be, and watch him use you!

QUESTIONS FOR PRAYER AND CONVERSATION

1. If your marriage fits into the Warrior woman–Artist man configuration, how have your personalities been either resisted or encouraged within the church?

2. If you are a Warrior, either male or female, how is God tempering your strength with humility to empower your marriage and your ministry?

3. If you are an Artist, either male or female, how is God adding courage to your creativity to empower your marriage and your ministry?

BUILDING ON THE PAST

How to Honor the Generations

THORPE WAS SITTING across from me (Jerome) this morning. His face still held a shadow from his disappointing show in the city swim meet. At eight years old, Thorpe is large for his age and naturally athletic. But he has been on the swim team for only six weeks, and he was swimming against kids who have been at it for years. He was taking it hard, and I couldn't blame him. It's tough to lose in competition.

As I tried to give Thorpe a larger perspective on the situation, I described how my childhood had been quite different from his. I was small and notably unathletic all through grade school and didn't really catch up physically until I was in college. I tried to explain the hard truth that many people assign value to you based upon your performance in some field—

149

athletic, musical, academic. Or they judge you based on physical beauty, social grace, or some other external standard.

I suspect Thorpe will have it easier than I did, at least in sports. My dad grew up small but determined, making a place for himself as a 130-pound guard on the high-school football team. For Dad, it was all about guts! But in college, he excelled in both wrestling and gymnastics, and he remains a lifelong runner. Still, as I grew up, team sports did not have a high value in our home, and I didn't make any teams in my school. Now that Kellie and I have kids, we want to give them the chance to try different sports and find one they can pursue if they wish. Knowing how much to push them and how much to let them choose for themselves can be a fine line.

We're trying to coach all three of our children through the seasons of life and all the changes each season brings. We're trying, just as our parents did, to lay a foundation of values and character that will serve them well as they grow up and discover their own destiny. We try to convey to them the things we have learned along the way—the value of hard work, the value of relationships, the value of spiritual excellence as well as physical excellence—and yet give them opportunity to try new things, to fail and to succeed in their own spheres of interest.

This is the way it's supposed to be: one generation lays the groundwork for the next.

A Matter of Perspective

One of the challenges of writing a book—or living life, for that matter—is the tendency to become overly focused on the moment. The now is essential to walking with God, of course, but along with that we have to broaden our perspective in order to grasp God's larger view. God has the broadest perspective of all; he sees his entire work of redemption throughout human history...from Creation and the Fall through the millenniums that pass as his plan unfolds. God takes his people through one generation after another to reveal his heart and establish his Kingdom, to draw men and women into his Kingdom passion.

Here at the end of our book, we want to affirm that we have a multigenerational God who has a multigenerational vision. His vision is for his glory and his ways to be lived out in his people. He cherishes every generation and has a unique mission for every people in every time.

The beauty of generational connectedness is that even as you get older and a younger generation begins to take center stage, your role isn't over. The new generation needs the strength and wisdom of the prior generation. The older generation shifts into a mentoring role, helping the new generation fulfill its destiny. It's a powerful dynamic.

As the newer generation comes into its own, the older generation needs to see that the part they play in God's drama is built on the work of past players...and the players of the future will take what this generation accomplished to new heights in new ways.

God has an overarching perspective that we don't always have. Our generation wouldn't be where it is without the wisdom and work of the prior generation. But at the same time, we have heard God in a new way for our generation. It really is a progressive process of building God's Kingdom. The younger men and women of God may look, think, and act differently than we're comfortable with, but that's because we're not part of that generation. The challenge is not to disdain what God is doing today or what he has done in the past. Both the older and the current generations need to honor what God is doing, even when it differs from what he called our generation to do.

A Clean Hand-Off

During the last summer Olympics, it was obvious in the relays that it didn't matter which team had the fastest runners if they couldn't make the hand-off well. These men and women train day in, day out on something as simple as getting a little stick from one person's hand to the other person's hand…because there are so many opportunities for it to be dropped. The outcome of the race hangs largely upon that one transaction—a clean hand-off, the ability to give up at the right time and to receive at the right time. It involves communication and trust.

The same is true of the trust that is needed among God's children. The older generation needs to recognize that it doesn't have the last and best word on what God is doing, and those in the younger generation need to see that, without the foundations already laid for them, they would be starting at ground zero. They could never accomplish their destiny in God. They must honor what has been given to them, acknowledging the sacrifices made and the Kingdom work already accomplished. And that's tough for younger generations. It's not characteristic of youth to see as broadly or to be as appreciative, and because of that, there is a tendency to take for granted things that were purchased at great cost to others and then given freely to their generation.

No generation is perfect, of course, but with the generation that is now rising, there are signs that God is doing something really different and significant. There is a higher level of expectancy for new things. It feels like the generational shift is bigger this time.

This helps explain why there has been so much discussion and writing about the shift from modernism to postmodernism. Some Christians consider *postmodernism* a bad word or a bad concept, but it's a reality that can't be avoided. The world is changing—in some ways for the worse and in some ways for the better. The body of Christ has the challenge and opportunity, as always, to release a new generation and let it do and be what God intends in the present day.

The rub between generations is accentuated because this shift is so monumental; worldviews and values are being deconstructed and reconstructed on such a large scale. This is a time not to hold on to old values just because they are old and not to embrace new values just because they are new. It's a time to know who God is and what he's doing, the older and younger generations together. It's time for the generations to step into unity, recognizing that each generation has had and will have its unique callings and passions—to complement what came before. Respect and honor need to flow in both directions, up and down the generational lines.

The Good Fight of Faith

Christian couples face a very real spiritual foe, an Enemy that understands the power that is released in the Kingdom of God when generations come into agreement. He does everything he can to sever one generation from another. He accentuates their differences and introduces subtle competition; he amplifies minor offenses and erects barriers to prevent generations from moving in harmony. But the Spirit of God overcomes such demonic intentions, overcomes our own flesh and selfcenteredness, and allows us to link arms between the generations and advance his purposes together.

Speaker and author Graham Cooke likes to say a "good fight" is one that you win! Our battle is not against any generation. Our battle, as always, is against spiritual forces that seek to divide and conquer. But this is one fight we can win! Love is the call; truth is the charge; unity is the challenge of the generations.

This vision requires a lot of trust. As the prior generation recognizes

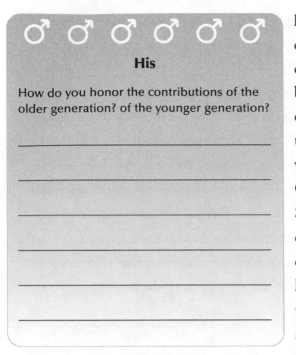

His

How do you honor the contributions of the older generation? of the younger generation?

_____

_____

_____

_____

_____

_____

how the values are shifting, it's easy for them to feel that the core of the Christian faith is being compromised just because current expressions of the faith look so different. But we're still worshiping the same God and following the same Spirit. Although God doesn't change, his strategies do change; the Bible is a record of how they have changed over time. Yet God's character remains constant. Those who can move with God and navigate the inevitable changes will remain at the center of what he is doing. These are the people who get to partner with God on the earth.

Think of what has happened in the area of worship as a microcosm of this dynamic. The last forty years have seen a major shift from what we would call traditional worship styles, mainly anchored in hymns and pipe organs, into contemporary worship, with new songs and new musical instruments. For many, it has been a highly emotional struggle to see how God could be honored and exalted by a soaring electric guitar! And yet, wise men and women in both generations can recognize the beauty of God displayed in both expressions of worship.

I (Jerome) lead a worship band full of teenagers, and they express themselves in the musical language of today. That's the authentic form for them to convey their passion for God. But the last time I led worship, we played all hymns—modern arrangements of timeless classics. And there was a real sense of spiritual authority in that because, for forty-five minutes, we bridged the generations.

When we talk about how each generation needs the other, we're really talking about partnership. Partnership is essential between husband and wife, but it extends far beyond marriage into all of life. It extends into the church, into the workplace, into the culture…and it extends into generations. We have to see the generations partner with one another and release the same authority from their unity that is released in the oneness of marriage. God's authority flows through people who come into agreement and mutual respect, who share a common purpose and a common passion. God has said he will bless the place where his people live in unity (see Psalm 133). He will make that unity the beacon that shines his glory upon the entire earth! We need to understand and emphasize how much we need one another in the Body of Christ.

Kellie and I don't think it's an accident that we were born right on the division line between the Boomers and the Busters. That has purpose to it. And part of that purpose, we believe, is a calling to bridge the generations, to encourage unity among them. We want to explain one generation to the other and help the generations

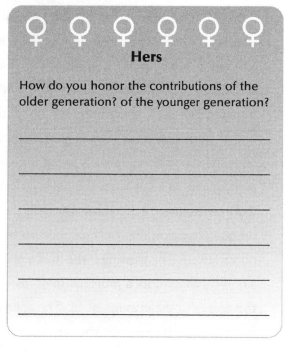

Hers

How do you honor the contributions of the older generation? of the younger generation?

_____

_____

_____

_____

_____

_____

to honor each other. In this book we're trying to set fresh perspectives for both generations. Set on the anchors of a biblical vision for marriage, we want to affirm God's unceasing mandate to women and men since time began and to encourage every couple to navigate those biblical passages in ways that are real and authentic in their generation. We particularly want to release the new generation from unnecessary or unbiblical boundaries on how marriage is expressed, speaking a word of freedom for them to discover an equal partnership and a one-flesh destiny.

The Chance to Bless

By reading the Scriptures, you can grasp a larger perspective on the passage of time, traversing generations in minutes as you read of one generation laying the groundwork for the next. One of the things that stands out is how vital it was, and is, for the older generation to bless the younger. Time after time when one generation was ready to enter heaven, there would be a laying of hands upon the heads of the children to impart the blessing, the affirmation, the empowerment for the new generation. It really highlights something of the Father's heart for his children, for all of us.

At times that must have been difficult for our spiritual ancestors. The new generation wasn't always living out the vision in the same way their parents had. In some cases the older generation was more faithful to God than the younger generation. But still they passed on the blessing. It's a unique possession that only parents can bestow…and for children there is no substitute. The blessing is the final seal of partnership. Of course, it's not a one-time event; it's a progression of many acts, words, and attitudes over the years that conveys approval. The approval isn't for every decision that is made; it's a blessing for the next generation *as people*—people who are

Godward in their passion and living out their generational purpose to the best of their ability.

And the blessing goes back up the line too! Parents need the affirmation and appreciation and validation that come uniquely from their offspring. This is where partnership comes full circle, breaking generational bondages and advancing God's Kingdom on planet Earth.

God's authority is released in unity. When the generations honor and bless one another, they will be able to come together to serve the Kingdom. And they will experience the Kingdom-advancing, world-transforming authority of God like never before. This is our heartfelt vision.

QUESTIONS FOR PRAYER AND CONVERSATION

1. Is your perspective wide enough to recognize and affirm the expressions of God in each generation?

2. How can you improve the hand-off between your generation and the next?

3. How can you communicate blessing up and down the generational lines?

Dusk

A wisp of hope upon the shadowed mind
She turns and lifts the corners of her lips
A smile flits and dances 'cross the time
Between the kiss of glance and glance of kiss

Now caught before the glance can go amiss
She yields to touch that plucks a weary sigh
Within the harbor of my longing 'brace
We rest inside the eddy of the mind

Though hungry for the melding of the soul
A host of other calls rend us apart
While serving sends the mind upon the sole
We turn to task sustained with lifted heart

And as the twilight bends the day to night
Her fragrance warms my heart like firelight

NOTES

1. It is interesting that both genders are needed to represent God's image, which highlights the dysfunction of homosexuality.
2. All poetry by Jerome Daley.
3. Adapted from Jimmy Evans, *Marriage on the Rock: God's Design for Your Dream Marriage* (Amarillo, TX: Majestic Media, 1994), 270.
4. Loren Cunningham and David Joel Hamilton with Janice Rogers, *Why Not Women? A Fresh Look at Scripture on Women in Missions, Ministry, and Leadership* (Seattle: YWAM Publishing, 2000), 96.
5. Cunningham and Hamilton with Rogers, *Why Not Women?* 96.
6. Cunningham and Hamilton with Rogers, *Why Not Women?* 98.
7. For examples in Scripture of God's feminine form of self-expression, see Isaiah 49:15; 66:12–13; Psalm 131:2; Proverbs 1:20–33; 3:13–20; 4:5–9; 8:1–9:12.
8. For more information on the ministry of Jerome and Kellie, visit www.onefleshministries.org or www.purposecoach.net.
9. For more on "waiting seasons," read *When God Waits* (WaterBrook, 2005) by Jerome Daley.
10. Attributed to "The Good Wife's Guide," *Housekeeping Monthly,* May 13, 1955.
11. Aristotle *The Generation of Animals* 1.20.728a18–21, quoted in Cunningham and Hamilton with Rogers, *Why Not Women?* 77.
12. B. Bava Batra, *The Talmud,* 58a, quoted in Cunningham and Hamilton with Rogers, *Why Not Women?* 102–3.
13. Cunningham and Hamilton with Rogers, *Why Not Women?* 109.

14. For the most thorough and scholarly work on equality, we recommend Ronald W. Pierce and Rebecca Merrill Groothuis, gen. eds., *Discovering Biblical Equality: Complementarity Without Hierarchy* (Downers Grove, IL: InterVarsity, 2004).

15. Jordan Paul and Margaret Paul, *Do I Have to Give Up Me to Be Loved by You?* (Center City, MN: Hazelden, 2002), 7–12.

16. This idea is drawn from Paul and Paul, *Do I Have to Give Up Me to Be Loved by You?* 9, 13.

helm, norm:

ID	author	title
72	grippando	under cover of darkness
151	grippando	when darkness falls
231	grisham	appeal
430	groff	monsters of templeton
427	gross	reckless
317	gruber	book of air and shadows
375	haddam	living witness
408	haig	capital game
410	haig	hunted
393	haig	kingmaker
392	haig	mortal allies

To learn more about WaterBrook Press and view
our catalog of products, log on to our Web site:
www.waterbrookpress.com

WATERBROOK
PRESS